Gaps and Bridges

NORMAN H. FULTON

Fulton Books, Inc.
Meadville, PA

Published by Fulton Books 2021

ISBN 978-1-63710-007-3 (paperback)
ISBN 978-1-63710-009-7 (hardcover)
ISBN 978-1-63710-008-0 (digital)

Printed in the United States of America

To my family with much love and to
incarcerated children everywhere.

CONTENTS

Memorial in the center of town

I became involved with the civil rights movement, from the time Medgar Evers was murdered to my present time and working with incarcerated kids, that I understand how some people simply do not get their fair share of our country's wealth. In all probability, some of them never will never get their fair share unless we change our perception of the inner city. I love our country, and I feel strongly that it is the best form of government in the world today if it is administered correctly. Everyone is equal; each of us has a voice, an opportunity for success. People are slow to realize that we are a republic, and on election day, we entrust our bill of rights and constitution to politicians, and many of them seem to be incapable of doing the job. My heart aches for the politician who is dedicated to doing his or her best to serve the nation and is blocked by political squabbles.

In my book *Gaps and Bridges*, I compare growing up in Pine Plains, a small town in New York, to the inner city of New York. It covers a span of the '60s to the '20s. My research consisted of interviewing teachers who have taught in a small town and those who are teaching in the inner cities, plus the 2,500+ incarcerated kids I have worked with during the past eleven years, 85 percent of whom are minorities. Put them all together, and the conclusion is that far too many inner-city schools are failures. But we seem to lack the courage, understanding, and compassion to change negatives to positives in a civilized and caring way.

In 1992, I was ordained a deacon in the Episcopal Church at the Cathedral of St. John the Divine in NYC (the largest Gothic cathedral in the world.) Deacons and priests are equal orders, but we occupy different ecclesiastical space. Deacons serve at the altar and are expected to bring the world into the church and the church into the world, and when we are in the world, we are expected to look for the Christ or good in all people. In thirty years of ministry, it does exist in all people, but it takes patience and love to find it. We have done an excellent job of addressing women, gay and civil rights, and hunger issues. However, I'm saddened that the cause, in too many cases, has blotted out the teachings of Jesus Christ. The stories you will read are infuriating and sickening as our country has seemingly turned its back on the kids at risk. All the names have been changed to protect the children and people I interviewed and the places I visited.

CHAPTER 1

Beginning Gaps

Having grown up in a small town and volunteering in the inner city, I became intrigued and bothered by the differences between small-town America and inner-city America. This book is intended to examine that and call attention to the wide gap in education between the inner city of New York and the northern suburbs and the damage it is doing to our kids. When I attended seminary in New York City, I spent a couple of days in Bedford-Stuyvesant, a very depressed part of the city. I learned firsthand about one school that didn't have the necessary supplies to have a meaningful class—broken blackboards, no chalk, and pathetic books. At first, I thought this is an easy fix—we raise some money and buy everything they need, and the problem is over. But it's not. First, you have to get a big cauldron and mix in a "who cares?" attitude, bumbling incompetence, and the lack of oversight and sprinkle it all with a little racism. The kids at the end of their time in one Bed-Stuy school were given a certificate of attendance, not a certificate of graduation, and most of the certificates were lies as they gave the illusion that the kids received some kind of education. The people in the neighborhood got rid of the City Board of Education and replaced it with their own people. They harassed men coming into the neighborhood looking for prostitutes or trying to turn their children into prostitutes. Once they saw a car with out-of-town license plates, they identified who the man was and sent a letter to his wife and family explaining what he was doing. It wasn't a legal exercise, but when it comes to protecting your children, it's hard to find fault. One man said, "I'm sure that some poor guy was in the area to do nothing more than to pick up a loaf of bread. He added, "But f— him." Such was the depth of frustration about their schools.

Today, twenty-five years after that visit to Bed-Stuy, the kids in the inner city and jail still fuel my civil rights walk. Every morning when I have breakfast, a Bible verse pops up on my iPad, and that puts me in touch with the divine. Today, it was from the book of Psalms (84:11) that read in part, "He withholds no good thing from those who have integrity." I wondered if He withheld anything from the people in Bed-Stuy or me. A couple of sips of coffee and I flatter myself by concluding, *No, He wouldn't hold anything from me, as I have plenty of integrity*. It's not completely true, but it's a comforting thought for the day. Regardless, it prompts time for reflection about what am I doing with my life. Then the word of the day pops up. Today was "senescence," the process of becoming old. Most of the time, growing older is wonderful. It gives me a chance to look back over my life and wonder why I thought things that seemed so important at the time are now seen for what they were, stepping stones to more knowledge. All of what happened creates a mosaic of my life, and I become almost godlike, with the ability to see the whole picture and not focus on some nonsensical problem that occupied so much of my time. Once my morning ritual is completed, I scan the *Wall Street Journal, New York Post*, and *The Journal News*. Most of the news is not good, and in 2019–2020, it would appear that everyone hates someone, and in particular political races have morphed into who can dig up the most dirt on their opponent without any plan to improve life on good ole Mother Earth, and people suffer because they don't realize what good things can be done.

A friend of mine grew up in the projects in the South Bronx and said, "You would be surprised how many people never get to Manhattan. I was lucky because I had a strong mom. When I got into trouble, she sent me to stay with a family in South Carolina. She taught me the value of working, and because of that, I got an internship with a large company in midtown Manhattan. I was seventeen years old, and our holiday party was at the Guggenheim Museum. All I could say was "Wow." Is this the way people live? Is this how they celebrate? Living in the projects, I never saw anything like it. I knew that I didn't want to stay in the projects. It all started because of the work ethic instilled in me by my mother and my first job at Burger King, which gave me exposure to other things. If you stay in the projects and you don't have anyone in your corner, the chances are you will get into trouble. If you never leave the hood, you won't know what you don't know, and you are trapped in the projects.

After I served twenty years in the Big Brothers Big Sisters program and youth sport programs, I started to develop an interest in kids who were at risk. I've been volunteering for the kids in jail for ten years, and I'm honored that over 2,500+ kids have attended my classes. My involvement started simply enough. I had helped with a couple of projects at the jail, and one day, there was a message on my phone, saying, "Mr. Fulton, this is Sarah at the Secure Detention Center, and we would like you to be our guest speaker for Black History Month." I was honored but surprised. I called them to confirm, and when I tried to ask a question, she said, "You sound a little hesitant. Are you okay with this?" I responded by saying, "I just want to make sure," and before I went any further, she had said, "Oh, Mr. Fulton, we know that you are White." I went and I spoke to them about one of the greats in civil rights, Medgar Evers. As a deacon in the Episcopal Church, I felt that I had to pray, and at the end of my talk, I asked the kids to stand and gather in a circle. That caused some concern with the security guards, but the social worker felt that it was okay. I gave the kids the option to hold hands, and I was impressed that they all did so with the exception of one who was twelve years old. When he saw that the other kids were holding hands, he said, "Okay, I'm secure enough in my manhood. I'll do it." Everybody smiled at that. I told the kids that they didn't have to pray, but if they liked, they could just tell me who they want prayers said for. After the first request, the floodgates opened, and the requests came fast and furious: "I would like a prayer for my mother. I know the bastard is beating her." "Pray for my brother. He's really messed up." "Please pray for my court appearance. My girlfriend is messed up on drugs, but I still love her." All the kids in that room asked for a prayer that provided a glimpse into the understanding of life and the gaps that were crushing these kids. The majority asked for prayers, not for themselves, but for the needs of others in a sensitive and caring way. Few people realize that a fair number of these kids go to church. Their church may not be in the traditional sense of a church, but rather a storefront church or a room in an empty building. God bless those people, specifically grandmothers who are doing their best to keep the church alive in these kids' lives.

The more I became involved with kids in jail, I found I was becoming their advocate and I was changing. More and more, I was speaking on their behalf and meeting with people like the Honorable Janet DiFiore, DA of Westchester about these kids. I finally realized how much I changed when a person said, "Norm, your problem with kids in jail is that you have become a bleeding-heart liberal." I was changing, and more and more, I was honored by the comment. After working hard with the disadvantaged, counseling those who need help and families impacted by HIV/AIDS, I think of myself as a Christian who loves a good cause.

CHAPTER 2

What Gap?

All through high school in Pine Plains, I knew of maybe one kid who was sent to a juvenile detention center. In the inner city, it's a way of life. Why is that? In Charles Krauthammer's book *The Point of It All*, he talks about the gap as a great way to measure who is the greatest. For example, in 1921, Babe Ruth hit fifty-nine home runs more than half the teams in the major leagues. In the 1981–1982 hockey season, Wayne Gretsky scored 212 points. The next two guys scored 147 and 139. Mr. Krauthammer, after applying his gap measurement, declares Tiger Woods is the greatest golfer who ever lived. Mr. Krauthammer writes, "Of the last eleven majors, Woods has won seven." That means that whenever and wherever the greatest players in the world gather, Woods wins twice, and the third trophy is distributed among the next 150 or so. Secretariat, at the Belmont, hit the finish line thirty-one lengths ahead of the next horse, and Bobby Fischer had the same gap when he played chess. In my own humble opinion, Babe Ruth was the greatest champion of all as he changed baseball and the country. His teammate, Harry Heilmann, said of Babe, "Sometimes I can't believe what I saw. This nineteen-year-old kid, crude, poorly educated, only lightly brushed by the social veneer we call civilization, gradually transformed into the idol of American youth and the symbol of baseball to the world over—a man loved by more people and with an intensity of feeling that perhaps has never been equaled before or since." To me, Babe's biggest contribution was that he demonstrated what kids from the inner city could do when given a chance.

These gaps are easy to measure: I hit five home runs, you hit three, so the gap is two. I'm the best. But in day-to-day life, it's impossible to measure the gap. I was at the mall, and I watched a woman with three kids in tow and carrying one in her arms. They were standing at a fast-food outlet. One of the kids was crying because he didn't get what he wanted. She leaned over, smiled, and spoke to him. He calmed down. She never missed a beat, the mustard and ketchup containers were filled, and off they went to find a table. I've seen other mothers in a similar position scream at their kids to get them to stop annoying her. Between the screamer and the cool one, there would appear to be a huge gap. The cool one goes into the pantheon of champions or at the very least the Hall of Fame for mothers.

I have talked to people who were born and raised in the inner city, and I hear about women who work two or three jobs to put food on the table and work very hard to keep their kids out of trouble. They never get any publicity. How do you compare her to a person that is on the front page of newspapers because a person made a gift of thousands? To be sure, donations are vital to nonprofits and God bless them. One gives from her wallet, the other from her heart. How do you measure the gap? How do you measure the gap between a teenager forced into drugs and prostitution and the suburbs where good things are available?

Nowhere is the gap more obvious than with kids in jail. They are expanding the secure detention center where I volunteer as they are now transferring seventeen-year-old kids from the adult jail to the youth jail. Overwhelmingly, they are a great group of kids, and with a break here and there, they wouldn't be in jail. About 85 percent of the kids are the minority, and if you have an IQ above one hundred or if you have one iota of caring about minority children, you have to wonder why. The truth is that most people do care, but with all the stories about gangs, they are concerned about their safety. To help bridge that gap, I asked a couple of people to come with me to the jail, and it was a disaster. One White guy tried his best to act like he was just a "bro" from the inner city. It was embarrassing. Another person said, "I don't feel comfortable being with these kids." There was a hint of racism, but when we talked about it, she was okay. It wasn't the color but just the fact she was having a problem being with criminals. She was simply being honest. The third person looked into a cell and saw a twelve-year-old boy of color sitting on the edge of his bed. He backed away from the cell and stood there and cried. I liked him. He saw a child in need of help. He didn't come back, but he pledged support, and he kept his word. With another group, Lori, a woman of color, prominent in the community, looked at all the kids of color and said, "My God, what are we doing to my people?" I never forgot the look on her face or that statement, but what are we doing to kids of color in the inner city? Out of ignorance and lack of concern, we aren't doing much. I wish her family didn't move to California.

It must be mind-numbing for teenagers of colour in the inner city to read about **critical race theory (CRT)**, that their country is inherently racist and skip over the hundreds of laws that have been passed to ensure equality. The editors of the *Encyclopedia Britannica* describe CRT as,

> "an intellectual movement and loosely orga-
> nized framework of legal analysis based on the
> premise that race is not a natural, biologically
> grounded feature of physically distinct subgroups
> of human beings but a socially constructed (cul-
> turally invented) category that is used to oppress
> and exploit people of colour. Critical race theo-
> rists hold that the law and legal institutions in
> the United States are inherently racist insofar as
> they function to create and maintain social, eco-
> nomic, and political inequalities between whites
> and nonwhites, especially African Americans."

I understand the point that if you raise two children of different color, they will not be racists. Since the government is the people, how does racism start? It's easy to blame the government when *we* are the problem.

Stissing Mountain

Forgotten Gaps

I should point out that there are a number of wonderful families in the inner cities, but many times, they are buried under an onslaught of societal problems and are worn down. There is no gap between the inner city and the suburbs when it comes to the desire to love and care for their family and a desire for needful things.

Beth wrote to me and said, "Growing up in Pine Plains was like living in a cocoon of family and friends. Everyone knew you, your parents, where you lived, and what church you went to. Wherever you went in town, you would see someone you knew, and you would be greeted by name. There was a familiarity that resulted in feelings of security and safety."

However, we were not safe. The world of evil found us. In the '60s, in ten short years, Medgar Evers, John F. Kennedy, Robert Kennedy, and Martin Luther King were assassinated. The Vietnam war was built on lies, and we believed what Presidents Kennedy, Johnson, and Nixon told us about Vietnam. Nixon took it up a notch and taught us about corruption and how to lie on such a high level it brought down the presidency. Ten miles from our town of Pine Plains, Timothy Leary brought LSD into the world and asked us to turn off and turn on. And why not, Black churches in the south were being firebombed, and Americans were horrified to see American Black people being fire hosed and shot because they dared to ask for basic liberties. I visited one church in Birmingham that was bombed. The Sunday school took the biggest hit, and four young girls were killed and others injured. That does not include psychological damage. Many young people became disgusted with the government and demonstrated to end the war in Vietnam. When Muhammad Ali was drafted into the Army, he said, "I ain't got no argument with no Viet Cong," and refused to be drafted." That phrase echoed through every town in America. It all came to head when on May 4, 1970, during a peace demonstration, four students were killed and nine others were wounded at Kent State University by the Ohio National Guard. They were protesting the expansion of the war into Cambodia and the presence of the National Guard on campus. Our country was spinning of control, and for the lack of a better vocabulary, it was pure evil.

Churches and others in the USA rushed in to stem the tide of evil. But many big churches of all denominations started to lose their way and became pseudo politicians. They made a sharp turn to the left and left many rural towns to wonder what happened to the Bible stories and teachings they cherished. On the right stood the hate groups masquerading as religious people. Most of the centrists disappeared. Through it all, the small towns with churches and farms stood the tallest in the fight against evil but our society started to falter under the onslaught of evil such as drug and sex trafficking. Our leaders seem to be so frustrated by civil disobedience that they started making outrageous comments on social media and the at-risk the kids were watching and taking it all in and they are confused. Drug cartels and gangs offer their own solutions which for many is quite attractive.

So with this background of societal change and anger and hatred, what do we do to reduce juvenile crime? In jail, I asked a class, "Okay, guys, what do we do to reduce juvenile crime?" Jamal, a fifteen-year-old with limited education and built like an oak tree said, "Hey, yo. Yo, Mr. Fulton, I know how to do it. First, you sell this jail, the one at Coxsackie, and the one in Goshen." Immediately, without thought or any respect for Jamal's knowledge of the problem, I laughed and said, "Okay, Jamal, and how does this reduce crime?" Jamal said, "Take the money you make on the sale of these places and invest it in education in the hood. Until you do that, you ain't reducing no frigging crime." How many millions of dollars do we pay educators and politicians to solve this problem? Jamal understood. He sized up the problem and had a solution. Jamal is right; the key is education, education, and more education. I told Jamal that I underestimated him and apologized and added that I have talked to a number of influential people and that his answer about how to reduce juvenile crime was the best I had ever heard. Other people talk about social programs, etc., but I said to Jamal, "You summed it up in a few short sentences, and I'm going to talk about you and your answer wherever I go." He stood in front of the class and just glowed. These kids deserve all the praise and support we can give them

The education problem in the inner city can be fixed. I suggest that we put the problem in the hands of Corporate America and tell politicians to stay away. I don't want a donation from corporate; I want their minds and hands to do the planning as if they were working on a research and development project for their company and hopefully adopt the school as part of a five year plan. When everything is finished, then the politicians can come back and take the credit for the new schools in their district and how they reduced the crime rate. The consensus of the teachers is to teach kids what they need and can handle intellectually, not what the state says they need. One kid got angry when I asked, "How was your education?" and he said, "It sucked." And he asked, "Why can't we get the same things that the rich kids have in their schools?" I knew the answer, but at the time, I couldn't think of a good answer without fanning the winds of hatred and racism. What I felt like saying was "It's because you're getting screwed and too many people don't care." But I think he had figured it out already. With poor education kids cannot explore their purpose.

Stissing Lake and Mountain. We learned to swim and climb the tower

CHAPTER 4

Gaps Hurt

Not all things are joyous and happy when working with kids who are incarcerated. Sometimes you get frustrated by what you are hearing that you have to shed tears. These are some of the conversations with kids I will never forget.

After talking about conflict resolution without violence, I asked, "Who has been able to do that?" Susie said, "I have," and explained how she did it. "I told him to get his hands off me, and I told him again, and he didn't, so I stabbed him twice in the chest." I said, "Susie, that is not conflict resolution without violence." Her response was "Probably not, but he didn't bother me anymore." A couple of weeks later, I asked her, "What do you like to do?" and she said, "I love to write." I asked her to write something, and I would publish it in a newsletter. She did, and it was good. When the newsletter was printed, I brought it to the next class to show her, but unfortunately, she was being transferred to another facility. One of the security guards said, "She is probably in the courtyard. If you hurry, you can catch her."

There was Susie sitting in the back of a van with handcuffs on. The officer said he would give the newsletter to her. A couple of weeks later, I saw the same officer, and he told me that she read it and cried all the way to the next location. It was a sad day and I did cry and thought, *What a waste of life.* Two or three months later, I was walking across the common area, and I heard someone say, "Mr. Fulton." She got away from the guards and ran over and gave me the biggest hug I've ever had. Later, I thanked the security guards for not putting too much effort in to stop her.

Manuel told me that he was in the facility because he killed someone. He looked weak, and I said, "Are you playing me?" He looked me straight in the eye and said, "Nope, I stabbed him right in the heart." I was taken aback by how calm he was, and I asked him, "Was this a gang thing?" and he said, "Nope, just me." I said, "Look, there are things you should talk about just with your attorney." I loved his response, "Yeah, but ain't you some kind of clergy or something so you can't say anything even if you wanted to?" I told him, "That's true," and before he was able to get into full story, the security guards brought him back downstairs. He was transferred to another facility that night.

Lopez never said a word in two months. He was quiet and depressed. One week, when I came in, I was surprised to hear him say, "Hi, Mr. Fulton." The reason for his joy was that he saw his mother for the first time in two or three months.

Habib said, "They closed the center where we went to play games. It was a good safe place to go. The reason they did that was that they ran out of money, but they built a football field with artificial turf. I don't play sports. What kind of shit is that?"

One girl's advice to other girls was to get pregnant and have a baby. That baby is yours that you created. It's something you did and you can feel proud. Another girl said, "Please pray that I find a home that will love me and keep me safe." A similar prayer request has the same expectation that they wanted a prayer that they would not be hit.

Octavio asked if we could talk one-on-one. We did, and I asked him how his court case went. He said, "My attorney didn't really know who I was." When I asked if his family say anything to the judge, he said, "No one from my family was there; they forgot the date."

I asked one kid why he was there. I said, "I'm always interested in what happened, and if you don't wish to tell me, that's fine." He said for selling drugs. "What did your parents say?" He said, "My father is a drug dealer, and my mother is a f— whore. What do you think they said?" Reading between the lines, he was hoping and praying that they would say something to indicate they cared.

For the first time, I saw a boy cry in class. He spoke about how much his mother loves him and explained that the best time was when he washed the dishes with his mother; sometimes he would dry them. He said, "We talked about everything, and when we were done, my mother put her arm around me and told me how much she loved me. And then I was arrested and shamed her." Not one kid in class looked at him or spoke; there was dead silence because they knew how he felt.

Some kids struggle to say things. Primarily, they don't want to risk embarrassing themselves. I loved Tim because he didn't care; he just let it fly. He explained that he was thinking about taxes, and from the hoots in class, they thought he was a joke. He wanted to make a point that we should not tax people. I said, "How would you pay the soldiers and firemen?" The kids started to laugh. He said, "No, I don't mean that we shouldn't pay taxes. Aah, just forget it." I said, "You have something to say, so think about it, and let's start again." He said, "Let's say you make $200 and you need $150 to live on. They shouldn't tax the money you need, but just tax the $50." Nobody laughed—Tim for president.

I'll end this chapter with one of my favorite stories. In class, a kid handed me a slip of paper with a name and a phone number. I asked him, "Why are you giving me this?" He said, "It's my grandmother's name and phone number. She doesn't have enough money to post my bail, but I'm figuring you probably have enough, so if your call her and tell her that you will cover it, she can come to pick me up. When I get out and I finish high school and I get a job and I have a car, I'll send you a check." These kids always have their brain in overdrive. This is the crux of the no bail law in New York State: because he doesn't have money, he can't go home. But the no bail law should not apply to felons.

CHAPTER 5

Huge Gap
A+ for Intelligence,
D for Knowledge

I never took much time to think about white privilege, but it does exist. Peggy McIntosh, an associate director at Wellesley College, wrote a paper on White privilege. I hated it because the more I read it, the more uncomfortable I became. Peggy wrote that white privilege is like an invisible knapsack of special provisions, maps, passports, codebooks, visas, clothes, tools, and blank checks. She summed it up in fifty points. These are just a couple that should drive the point home; I can arrange to protect my children most of the time from people who may not like them; I can do well in a challenging situation without being called a credit to my race; and I can be pretty sure that if I ask to talk to the person in charge, I will be facing a person of my race. From personal experience, I can attest to the fact that all of this true. Then take a couple of more steps and mix her points with financial disparity, mixed up with discrimination, caused by financial disparity, and it gets lost. Soon you hear, "Look, I worked hard for what I have, the Black people should pull themselves up by their bootstraps, and they can have the same things I have." The big misunderstanding is that too many people do not have bootstraps.

When my wife who is an excellent paralegal came home and said she was working with a team of lawyers on a desegregation case, I jokingly said, "Has the office been transferred to Selma?" She said,

"No, it's in Yonkers, New York, just thirty miles south of where we are." A lot of good things came out of that case, and I believe the majority of people felt it was financial discrimination, not racism, that was denying Blacks the homes they desire. Of course, for many, racism caused the problem to begin with. Today, Yonkers is on the move upward, and it has become a great city. However, when discrimination, either racial or financial, is a reality, where do the kids get their life experience, and whom are they exposed to as role models?

Incarceration offers kids a never-ending supply of the wrong heroes. What better place to find the worst hero than in jail? In the early years of being at the jail, I commented on how wonderful a couple of the kids were and what a pleasure it was to have them in class. I later found out that they were there for attempted murder. Even more surprising was that some of the kids were asking for their autographs because they thought that someday they would commit a big-time crime. I talked to one kid about the future, and he said, "I ain't taking no job flipping no burgers at McDonald's." I said, "Actually, they are a great company to work for. They provide benefits, good salary, and educational opportunities." So, he said, "Hey, yo, look, I make $40,000 a year selling dime bags. Is McDonald's going to match that?" I said, "Yes, when you consider you are going to be incarcerated for a year. You lose $40,000 for the year, and you are left with zero, plus a record." There was no answer. A drug dealer was his big hero. Kids in jail don't think about or even fathom things like pensions, savings accounts, or investing in the stock market. The country should listen more to top farmers and countryfolk for solutions to juvenile delinquency.

Growing up in Pine Plains, there was a number of heroes, but they were not well known. The heroes were primarily the farmers and small-business owners who provided kids and some teachers who were off for the summer with part-time jobs and summer jobs. Now many of the farms are being gobbled up by big business; I fear that one of the cornerstones of our country is eroding faster than we think, and that is a big ripple of destruction.

Future Farmers of America Fair

CHAPTER 6

No Gap with Archbishop Tutu

What we need is a whole bunch of Archbishop Tutus. A number of years ago, Archbishop Tutu was a guest speaker at an event being put on by St. Peter's in Peekskill, NY. For those of you not familiar with Archbishop Tutu, he is a South African Anglican cleric and theologian known for his work as an anti-apartheid and human rights activist. He was the Bishop of Johannesburg from 1985 to 1986 and then the Archbishop of Cape Town from 1986 to 1996, in both cases being the first Black African to hold the position. Theologically, he sought to fuse ideas from Black theology with African theology. He emerged as one of South Africa's most prominent anti-apartheid activists. Although warning the National Party government that anger at apartheid would lead to racial violence, as an activist, he stressed nonviolent protest and foreign economic pressure to bring about universal suffrage (from Wikipedia). I am proud that IBM and a company called Texaco led the way.

I was pleased and surprised when I was asked to plan his day and accompany him while he was in Westchester. When I went to his hotel door, I really wasn't sure what to expect, and he quickly put any concerns I had to rest. With a big smile, he said, "Deacon Norm, how nice of you to take time to come to see me and make sure I get to the event. Sit down over here, and I want to hear all about your ministry." Humble and kind do not begin to describe him. We talked for about thirty to sixty minutes, and I gave him a briefing book about times and where he was to be. When we got downstairs, I said, "The Westchester County Executive is here, and a couple of

29

senators would like to meet you." He said, "I saw that in the briefing book, but first, I want to go to the kitchen," and off we went. When the door to the kitchen opened, the cooks and waitstaff seemed to all yell in unison, "Bishop Tutu, you didn't forget us!" He understood completely what it was like to be forgotten. He asked them numerous questions: "Is your family okay with you being out late tonight?" "Do they pay a good salary for working tonight?" and "Please thank your family for sharing you with me." He wanted to know what they were cooking and looked into each pot; he blessed them, and when we left, they were still talking in loud excited voices.

When we got in the hall, I said to him that there was a young lady working at the check-in table who would like to meet him and if possible have her picture taken with him. Three seconds later, a waiter was sent to get Karen. Introductions were made, pictures were taken, and then he said, "Karen, I can never find my table during these dinners. Would you do me a favor and let me take your arm and lead me to my table?" I think Karen was still smiling. He treated everyone with the utmost respect. With Archbishop Tutu, I quickly learned that when you were with him, it's most important to enjoy the moment, as people like Archbishop Tutu enter your life just once. These are some of his sayings that are so important in my work with kids who are incarcerated:

1. Differences are not intended to separate, to alienate. We are different precisely in order to realize our need of one another."
2. We may be surprised at the people we find in heaven. God has a soft spot for sinners. His standards are quite low.
3. Freedom and liberty lose out by default because good people are not vigilant.
4. Be nice to Whites; they need you to rediscover their humanity.

CHAPTER 7

Gaps of Frustration

I interviewed a number of wonderful people. Rosa taught in the inner city, and she is the perfect example of what a teacher should be—warm, caring, and intelligent. She told me how the kids in her class had to share a textbook. Give the book to Josiah on Monday, he gives it to Manuel on Wednesday, and on and on. Chances are she couldn't write on the blackboard, and once again, I heard that because the blackboard was broken, and if it wasn't, she still couldn't because there wasn't any chalk. I thought, *What do you think that did to the psyche of the kids and teachers?* She talked about how she had a part-time job in one of the wealthiest communities in Westchester County and how when she walked around the school. Rosa saw an endless display of the latest classroom equipment and books. Her reaction was one of the saddest things I have heard in researching this book. Rosa said, "I stood there and cried, and I couldn't stop." I usually have a comment, but words failed me completely. During a pause in the interview, she started to laugh most heartily, and I have to say, just to set the stage, she is a woman of color. She said, "Norm, don't you dare tell anyone I said this, or I will come after you, but President Trump is right. He is absolutely correct about what he is trying to do. What we need is schools of quality in the inner city that meet the needs of the kids. We don't have them because too many politicians are full of crap and the best they can do is to talk about it at election time." I hope Trump makes it. I quickly asked, "To be reelected?" And just as quick, Rosa said, "I didn't say that."

Frank Keppel, the first commissioner of education under President Kennedy, had a concern about the lack of education for poor children and said, "Education is too important to leave in the hands of educators." I suggest that we put it in the hands of Jamal; he was one of the few people who understood the problem and came to class with a solution.

Compare that with a teacher in the country. Beth, my friend and former neighbor, said that she remembered school as being traditional—books, desks in a row, workbooks, and "Raise your hand to speak."

She spent her teaching career in the area of early childhood education, working mostly with children four to six years old. She saw the beginning of the Head Start program and a realization of the importance of meeting the needs of young children. She added, "The focus turned to a developmentally appropriate approach. It moved away from the same workbooks and worksheets for everyone and focused on developmentally meeting the needs of the individual child at the place he or she was. This meant more variety of activities and more opportunities to experience, search, and learn through hands-on activities. It gave the child an opportunity to learn in various ways, not just through right or wrong answers on paper. Unfortunately, noneducators became involved in setting education programs and goals, and this child-centered type of learning is now being replaced by more focus on strict standards for learning and, in many cases, unrealistic expectations for children not ready for these standards. I am puzzled, disappointed, and dismayed by some of the activities and expectations I now see in classrooms for young children." She is a person who has sent out ripples from Pine Plains touching young students in a positive way.

Later in this book, you will be able to compare a country teacher to one who taught in the inner city and how there was a young man who was smoking a joint in class. She had him escorted out by the assistant principal. She thought he was gone for good. The next day, he waited for her outside of class and said, "You didn't think that you were getting rid of me?" and laughed. In my wildest thoughts, I can't imagine that happening in Pine Plains in the '50s or '60s. First, the other teachers and parents wouldn't allow it, and I would like to think that the students wouldn't allow it.

CHAPTER 8

Closed Gap

In 1960, the population of Pine Plains was 1,608; in 2016, it is estimated to be 2,422. Focusing on Pine Plains, the landmass is 30.59 square miles. Water inhabits 0.59 square miles, and the elevation is 474 feet. Crammed into this was the following:

1. Two doctors who made house calls
2. One movie theater
3. One shirt factory
4. One Ford dealership
5. One school that housed grades one through twelve
6. Three bars
7. Four restaurants and one pizza place
8. One funeral home
9. Three food markets
10. Three gas stations
11. One drugstore
12. One bank
13. Two dentists
14. One slaughterhouse
15. In the '50s and '60s, there were seventeen farms in the greater PP area. In 2020, there are now three.
16. One Black Angus farm
17. One newspaper (the *Register-Herald*)
18. Farm equipment dealer
19. One cemetery

20. One renowned maker of stained-glass windows
21. Local carpenters, electricians, and other trades
22. One part-time policeman
23. A great volunteer fire department

And in this small town, you knew all of them. If you screw up, everyone knew about it faster than Instagram could spread the news.

But in Pine Plains, the '60s was still a time when people said, "Thank you for doing that," and the other person would say, "You are welcome." Now, not so much. Now it's not unusual that "you are welcome" has been replaced with "no problem." Recently, when I was carrying a bundle and I said, "Thank you for holding the door for me," he said, "No problem. Don't worry about it." In Pine Plains, I believe that people volunteered as much as they do today. I don't remember that anyone called it volunteering. Church, youth group, in particular, played a big part in my life. There was no volunteering per se; we simply felt it was our Christian duty and I'm sure that my friends from the Jewish faith felt the same way. One day, my mother packaged up a box of food and clothes and told me to drop it off at the front door with the admonishment that it was not to be mentioned. She simply said, "They are up against it; there is no reason to embarrass them by talking about it to anyone."

My cousin Bill is the perfect example of a good student athlete living in the country. He is also my cousin and best friend. While Bill thrived in organized sports, I didn't like it, and much I preferred pickup games. Whatever the task, he dedicated himself to doing his best. I remember playing one-on-one in the back of the garage at dusk, and as usual, "I was winning," but I noticed that he would cut to the right, go to the corner, and shoot. I couldn't stop him. He kept saying, "Make it hard on me." Bill played on the varsity basketball team, and the next game—I think it was against Red Hook—he scored seventeen points. Guess where he shot from? I could see it coming, and I just smiled. I was so proud of him. Personally, I think I should have been given credit in the newspaper for half his points. With baseball, it's the same thing—just two of us. If you got a hit, the pitcher had to go get it. It was critical that the pitcher never take his eye off the ball so you could track it in the tall grass. Bill was on the JV baseball team; the next game, Bill went six for six. The next game, he was on the varsity.

Recently, I went to a high school football game, and I couldn't believe the equipment: a tower for the assistant coach and headphones so they could communicate with the head coach with some hot thoughts. In the late 50's/60's days, there was one coach for baseball, football, and basketball, as well as maybe one assistant, but no headphones and towers. Today, there are multiple coaches for everything. Coach Les Barton coached everything including summer baseball and even gym classes. There was no extraneous stuff, and it allowed him to focus on the game. Coach Barton is an interesting example of a teacher and community leader. Until I started writing this book, I didn't know that he was a major in World War II and was the commandant of headquarters in George S. Patton's Third Army Armored Division in 1939. As a coach, he has been enshrined in the Hall of Fame at Ithaca College and Dutchess County and the Pine Plains Wall of Fame. With the following record, he should be in Cooperstown. Remember that he never wore a headset and never climbed a tower.

As a multifaceted coach, he won seventeen league titles, ten county championships, and six Section I crowns as the boys' basketball coach at Pine Plains High School. His teams went 380-89 between 1939 and 1966 and set a state record with sixty-two straight wins. Barton also coached football for fourteen years, posting six undefeated seasons. In baseball, he won twenty-one league and county championships and started Pine Plains' first little league. In high school, I played one year of football for the coach. I got hit in the mouth that cracked the roots of my front teeth and decided this was not fun. But coach asked me to help coach a little league team with Irv. I didn't know why because I couldn't have been his favorite student athlete. When it was over, he sent me a letter of thanks. He saw something in me that nobody else did, and to this day, when I ask a student to do something, I go out of my way to thank them so they understand how important they are. He was a big ripple of good.

Shooting rats at the dump was popular. Picture this, there were five kids carrying loaded .22 caliber rifles walking down a road to a town dump that would be infested with rats, and for the next couple of hours, all you would be hearing was the sound of gunfire. Most remarkable was if someone had to put something in the dump, all shooting stopped, finger off the trigger, safety on, and rifles pointed up. There were no posted rules, just common sense, respect for each other, and following the rules sent to us by the NRA.

These are the people who I grew up with and are so protective of gun rights. Others were hunters who when hunting season opened went deer hunting. The meat was butchered and fed their family. I'm afraid that is a gap between city and country that will never be closed. People in the city are probably saying to themselves right now, "Why don't they just go to COSTCO?" The answer is cost savings, and people do like hunting. I doubt that none of the people I went shooting with will ever support people who say they need an AK47 or clips that hold extra rounds. Before we got a rifle, we received training materials from the NRA.

But why is it that mass shootings seem to happen primarily by white people in the suburbs? Once again, I turned to the wisdom of the kids in jail. I asked the class, "Why is it that mass shootings seem to happen in primarily White suburbs by White people, but never in the inner city?" Baptiste gave quite a unique and colorful answer. He said, "Hey, yo, Mr. Fulton, we would never do that where I live. If we had it in for somebody, we wouldn't go into a school and shoot everyone. We would wait until he came out and then put a cap in his ass." I said, "How about the drive-by shootings I read about?" He didn't have any real answer but just that it was a mistake and that should not have happened. Then I said, "What about the suburbs, Baptiste?" He got very serious and said, "Okay, hey, yo, Mr. Fulton, yo, no disrespect, but the reason it happens in the suburbs is because White people have a tight ass, no disrespect, okay? But y'all worry about your clothes and how you look, is your house big enough, you hate your frigging job, am I driving the right car? Some White people get so frustrated with all this they get a tight ass and then they go out and shoot people." Baptiste quickly added, "Okay, no disrespect, yo, no disrespect." I nodded and simply said, "No disrespect taken."

High School Agricultural Fair

CHAPTER 9

The Reverse Gap

Less than one percent of the population in Pine Plains were people of color. It just dawned on me that Irv who I mentioned in the previous chapter was a man of color. I believe the absence of people of color was caused by economic racism, which is subtle and vicious. I don't blame anyone for that, but there were no challenges to thoughts of white privilege and I suspect male privilege. But once you left the cocoon, there was a lot of baggage to unpack and discover your true beliefs. After high school, I took a bus ride to visit a friend in Miami, and I had my first encounter with racism. Somewhere outside of Charlotte, I sat across the aisle for a young girl of color. We made a rest stop; and three guys got on, with major beer bellies, looked at the girl, and said, "n—gger get in the back." I told her to stay where she was, and then I heard what people like Chaney, Goodman, and Schwerner probably heard. "Well, look what we have here, a N—— lover from the north." Chaney was from Mississippi and Goodman and Schwerner from NYC. They came to Mississippi to help Black people register to vote. They were murdered in August 1964 by the Klan, and their bodies were dumped in a landfill project. The story created an outrage in America that forced President Johnson to become personally involved. In 1988, a movie came out about this incident: *Mississippi Burning*. I would like to think that I would have had the courage to stand in front of her and protect her, but I had all I could to make myself look tough and not pee in my pants. I was spared that decision when the biggest bus driver I have ever seen got on the bus and said, "I want you, three slobs, off my bus." And they stopped walking up the aisle. As we drove on, I was dismayed that my feeble words were the only ones that were heard. A couple of years later, Medgar Evers was murdered (1963) by Byron De La Beckwith, and he was given a hometown parade. That was my welcome to civil rights. Every now and then, I think about what would have happened to me if the bus driver was delayed in getting back on the bus.

My small town didn't have that kind of impact of major news stories on the country, but Pine Plains did send out ripples across the land. For instance, one student became a colonel in the Air Force and touched our country in a positive way. Another became a member of the Presidential Ceremonial and Presidential Guards, another an attorney, and the beat went on: superintendent of schools, teachers, farmers, deacons, priests, speech pathologists, theater owners, real estate, tradesmen, and an author. Not too shabby for a small class in a small country town.

Today, I just read that Pine Plains sent out a big wave across our land that reached Syria. Shannon M. Kent, an honor student from my high school who spoke seven languages and a highly decorated Navy Chief Cryptologic Technician, was killed by a suicide bomber in Syria along with three other Americans. Flags have been lowered to half-staff to honor her. I stopped writing today to say a prayer of thanksgiving for her life and for strength and courage for her family. I can only imagine the size of the gap between Shannon and every other high school in America. There were five others who made the ultimate *sacrifice in Vietnam* from Pine Plains or attended high school from one of the hamlets around our town were:

- PFC James Joseph Lynch III
- PFC Jerry Alan Sweet
- PFC Bradley Joseph Simmons
- WO Peter Thomas Miller
- Peter Albertsen, Jr., AECS

In the inner city, thousands of people died fighting for their country.

Main Street in Pine Plains, still one traffic light

Who Knew from a Gap?

I went to grade school and high school in a very small town, Pine Plains and Stanfordville/Bangall, New York. In high school, there were sixty-seven kids in my class; in Stanfordville, there were two classes in one room. I loved grade school, and I couldn't wait to go to school. In high school, my grades went from the top to the bottom. It's not that I didn't like high school; I detested high school, and I was running out of excuses about how to cut a class, but I loved my classmates, many of whom I stay in touch with today. I loved college and graduate school. My wife knew me in high school, and she thought that I was bored. Apparently, I was bored and boring. She broke up with me, and I didn't see her for three years. The teachers were okay, but Mr. Lindsay DeGarmo was great. Somehow, he understood me completely. Once he took a group of honor students upstate to visit a historical site and he asked if I would like to go, I did, and it was a wonderful day. He was one of the finest men I have ever met. Shortly after high school, he died of cancer, then our next-door neighbor, and then my father; and my mother sunk into depression. And we lost out our home and most of our money. It was at the very least depressing. You wonder why things happen the way they do, but it was this experience that has helped me relate to the kids in jail. In one class, I opened up and spoke freely about losing our home and not having a great deal of money. I didn't realize it while I was talking, but when I looked around the room, the feeling from the kids was "he understands." That experience brings me closer to kids at risk.

Ms. Helen Wagner and Ms. Helen Hubbard were wonderful. Ms. Wagner had the study hall, a class scheduled in everyone's schedule. You went there to work on any subject you wanted to do, and Ms. Wagner would work with you. Ms. Wagner was knowledgeable of all the subjects and may have been the most intelligent person in high school. Writing this book, I remember Ms. Wagner walked a half-mile to get to my house. She told my parents that they have a wonderful son, but he could do so much better with his classwork. My father offered to drive her home, but she said, "No, thank you. I love to walk." I forgot about until now the gift she tried to give me. Ms. Hubbard was an English teacher, and I suspect a hopeless romantic. They were dedicated to education, and I always had the feeling that I could talk to them and that they understood. I still remained the same poor student, but I respected them. The business teacher had a wonderful sense of humor. During one of my detentions, we talked, and I don't know how, but I asked her if we could go out for lunch, or maybe, in a clumsy way, I was asking her for a date. She touched the side of my face and smiled. I understood, and she could not have handled that situation any better. Little did I know that the principal was listening to the whole thing and called me to the office. He was beyond angry and chewed me out about the lack of respect for a teacher. He could have played a recording of my last visit to his office. I told him that she was just being nice and was humoring me and it was not a big deal. I think while his eyes were bulging out of his head, he said something about how he would determine what was a big deal. I don't think he had any appreciation for romance. Try as I may, I can't remember any more conversations with her. I do remember the next day when I walked into class, I just sat down and thought nobody knew what happened, which was good. I never had another conversation with her. God only knows what the principal said to her.

Then there was one teacher and judge of all people without fear of contradiction. I'm sure somewhere he was a fine man, probably a good father and husband, but I couldn't stand the pompous ass. For example, once when I was walking home, he stopped his car, to talk to me. His wife and two daughters were with him. He asked me, "What are you doing?" I said nothing. "What are you going to do when you get to where you are going?" I said, "Probably nothing." "How about this evening? How about tomorrow?" Again, I said nothing. Then he said, "And that, Norman, is you. You are a nothing, and you will grow up to be a nothing; your whole life will be a nothing." And he drove off. The next day, he came up to me in the hall in school and said, "My wife felt that I was too hard on you and that I should apologize." Then he smiled with that miserable crooked smile, leaned forward, and whispered, "But I'm not going to." I said, "Good because it was nothing." I never forgot his comments. Once I was invited to speak at Westchester Community College, and my wife said, "That was very good. I wonder what your "favorite teacher" would be saying if he saw you." All these years passed by, and I can still recite all the words he said. That happened in a small town—what must it be like for a child of thirteen to be arrested and brought to jail in handcuffs? If comments from this teacher stuck with me, what sticks with these kids, and more importantly, would they be in jail if they had grown up in Pine Plains and not the inner city where gangs, drugs, and guns are so pervasive?

Going to grade school in Stanfordville, I don't remember that grade school had any of the latest equipment or textbooks, but there were two grades to a classroom. Looking back, I think we learned quite a bit from the "older kids" that supplemented the teachers. There was always a feeling of caring, and teachers asked about our families. And then came high school, and my grades went from the top to the bottom, and I was bored out of my mind.

I really don't understand why I just didn't click with what was going on. There were a couple of teachers that I truly loved and respected. Lindsay DeGarmo who was my math teacher was one of the finest teachers a student could have. But I failed math at every turn. I went to his house once to help him with a project, and when it was over, he said, "Don't you ever believe anyone who says you're not a hard worker and a good person." It was probably in reference to my dating Leslie who was a grade ahead of me and the salutatorian of her class. A teacher took her aside and told her not to date me as she could do much better. I remember Mr. DeGarmo took some honor students to the Albany area to tour a historic site, and I told him that I loved history and asked if I could go. He simply said, "That would be nice." It was one of my best days in high school.

Mr. DeGarmo and Leslie believed in me. After she graduated from college, she went to DC, and I lost track of her for three years. I wish the teacher who gave Leslie such dire warnings about dating me were alive a couple of years ago when Leslie and I celebrated our fifty-fifth wedding anniversary. She was and still is the greatest positive influence in my life.

There are positive influences in the inner city and in jail. I hear about loving and caring for family and boyfriends and girlfriends. But then they go back to the same negative influences.

High School

CHAPTER 11

Gaps and Ripples of Bad

From people who had a positive influence in my life, there are many kids who by birth have negative impacts in the inner city that Pine Plains has not experienced. One young incarcerated person's life was a disaster, and the following story illustrates the perfect way to keep the flow of juvenile delinquents coming into our society without any interruption

Ashganti said from jail, "I loved my mother, and sometimes I start feeling afraid because I may lose her. My father is a complete f—cking asshole. I hate him. In school, I was always bullied. I had enough and was determined to fight back and tried to stab a guy. I tried talking to my father about why I did it. He couldn't be bothered to talk about it. I was hoping for support. I told him some personal things that I never told anyone. I don't know why it came up, but I said, 'Why can't we have nice things?' The more I asked, the more pissed off he became. His answer was that he threw me out of the house and told me that he wants nothing to do with me. I hate the asshole. I ran outside and spent the next hour thinking about things I could do to hurt him. I was sent to a foster home, and I cried all night. My mother is sick, and I cried the entire night. I ran away. I was sent to two more homes and ran away. Finally, I had some more problems and ended up in jail. I do nothing but cry. When my mother needed me the most, I abandoned her, and I cry all the more. God, I hate this fuc—ing world."

If you feel that your community doesn't have enough juvenile delinquents and you like to raise one, this is a guide for families and communities about how to do it:

1. Make sure one of the parents, preferably the father, is not in the picture when raising children. Sometimes divorce is inevitable; but if it is to be, a raucous, hate-filled divorce filled with physical abuse is a good way, but even better is to mix in addiction to alcohol and drugs.
2. Abuse the children. Beating them is good; sexual abuse will have longer-lasting effects.
3. Scream at your kids. Whatever self-esteem they have, stomp on it. You might want to continually lay a guilt trip on them.
4. Constant fighting and screaming are good ways to abuse children, and it's important that you use all the filthy words you can think of. Call your wife a f——bitch or your husband a lazy bastard. Adding something like a useless bag of shit is good. This will give the kids an understanding of what awaits them when they grow up and that marriage should be avoided at all costs.
5. Make sure the school they attend is way below standard; never support the teachers. Put them down in front of the kids.
6. Make sure you never vote in local elections; that way, nobody can blame if nothing works.
7. Remove God from their life; that way, in their darkest moments, they will have nobody to turn to, and they will have no one when they need love and compassion the most.
8. For the community, it's simple: make life as difficult as possible for people of color; make sure they are excluded from everything, especially real estate, senior jobs, miserable grade school conditions, etc. Be creative; encourage kids to play video games about how to kill whores, police, etc. By now, the destruction of the child should be complete.

Patchin's Mill

CHAPTER 12

Gaps of Destruction

Rosa is a wonderful person—is bright, intelligent, and poised and has a wonderful sense of humor. I can see how children would be drawn to her. Rosa was raised in the segregated south and at an early age and had a desire to become a teacher. That started when she was in seventh grade. She had the most wonderful seventh-grade teacher. In the segregated south, there were not a lot of warm fuzzies from teachers for children of color. The big change in her life came when her family moved to the Lower East Side of Manhattan. Then it would be comparable to the South Bronx. Rosa went from segregation to integration, and she was completely lost. As a student, when she walked into class in NYC, the biggest thing Rosa remembered was when the teacher came over to her and gave her the biggest hug and said, "I am so happy to see you." The more Rosa thought about that hug, the more she knew than ever that she wanted to be a teacher and be just like her. She was wonderful. To Rosa, she was absolutely superb—all the more so because she was living on the Lower East Side of Manhattan, which then was the South Bronx, and I had just moved to New York City from the segregated south. Rosa, who just came from segregation and was thrown into integration, was totally lost.

Living in the Lower East Side, Rosa never saw so many kids that were ill-behaved and could care less about rules and manners. In the south, it was different. Most kids were well behaved and respectful of the parents and adults.

With this background, her teacher stood out like a shining star of hope. This teacher treated all students the same: She would give hugs, and she would give the brightest smiles to let us know that "You are here, and I see you," which was so important to Rosa. She made them feel important that there was no limit on what we could accomplish. From her, Rosa told herself, "I want to be a teacher. I want to be just like my seventh-grade physical education teacher." Rosa was inspired and majored in health and physical education so she could teach physical education.

Rosa explained that she started substituting in New York City in the mid-'70s; this is when the city went through its first financial crisis. She could say to my mother, "These are the worst kids I've ever seen in my life. I didn't know children could behave so bad." Her mother would say to her, "Well, if you find it this bad, I would rather let you go and get a job in a department store as a clerk or something instead of seeing you come home every day crying."

Despite her experiences through high school, Rosa stayed— partly because she was surrounded by a wonderful group of young teachers at that time and they formed a group. We helped each other to battle the everyday problems that we would have. Mostly the reason Rosa stayed was her courage and dedication to helping kids. Unfortunately, for Rosa, it was during this time that community school districts came into being, and while she hated saying it, a lot of people got their positions in administration through politics.

Consequently, some of them didn't even know what they were doing. A lot of schools went downhill. Children were not disciplined the way they were or should've been disciplined. Rosa remembered one day when the assistant principal in charge of getting substitute teachers in the school told her, "Just show up every day because someone would be out, and we will need you." That's what Rosa did.

I could tell from her body language that Rosa had a story to tell, and it was a dinger. Rosa told me, "I remember one day, the children came in from lunch because at that time, kids could go out for lunch. I was in the classroom waiting for them to come in. The students walked in; and this young man walked into the classroom, walked to the back of the classroom, took his seat, and proceeded to put his feet up on the desk. After he placed his feet on the desk, he took out a joint, and he lit it. Rosa was getting pumped up, saying, "Can you imagine this? This is in the back of my classroom while I'm in the classroom." This was in the seventh or eighth grade.

With a mixture of being flabbergasted and stunned, Rosa walked to the door of the classroom, and she called the students to come out in the hall and then sent one student to get the assistant principal. The assistant principal came in and escorted the young man out. Later on, the assistant principal said, "We need you to fill out some paperwork," and Rosa said, "Okay." Rosa was thinking this young man definitely would be suspended, his parents would be called in, and the situation would be taken care of. The next morning, when she went to work, standing in the classroom, Rosa saw the young man walking down the hallway toward her. Rosa was nervous about what was coming next. He looked at her and said, "You thought you were going to get me suspended, didn't you? You can't do anything to me." He just kept walking and laughing.

Again, during the interview, Rosa was still angry and incredulous that this young man sat in her class and had the temerity to smoke a joint in her class, knowing that nothing would happen to him. She still couldn't believe that this young man was caught and there were no consequences for his actions.

When Rosa went to lunch, her friends and fellow teachers were appalled, but not shocked. One of the more experienced teachers said that the principal would not allow him to be expelled, as it would not look good on her record. Above all, she was not going to waste an expulsion on a substitute teacher. A wonderful teacher with great potential was just given a knockout blow and never went back to that school again.

Despair

CHAPTER 13

Gaps: The Hell with It

While that was just one incident that happened in that school, Rosa kept pursuing her dream. When she reflected on the incident, she understood that the principal most likely did not want to have a high suspension rate because then it would look bad on her record and she had received that position politically, not earned that position. She wanted to shine, and it just brought the school down. The school was not a good school.

Looking at all this through the lens of a "country boy," I have the trouble grasping all this and translating it into prose that is fit for human consumption. There are kids not disciplined, books that are crap, the lack of supplies, and no sense planning on a new influx of supplies because the school budget doesn't cover such "luxuries." Where are the tax dollars? Where is the lotto money? Do you remember when people objected to introducing the lotto? The winning argument was "But all the money will go to support education." I think what they should have said, "If you're White, we have your back." I hope that's not true because there are a lot of good people doing their best.

Teachers were frustrated, Rosa was frustrated, the kids were frustrated, and dropping out Rosa was fuming that the classrooms were not stocked the way they should've been with papers, pens, chalk, and good books. When Rosa says good books, she means books for that particular subject that were not torn, were not marked into, and did not have graffiti on the front of the book cover. Books that are clean, so when you hand a book to a student, it's a clean book. A good principal and board would have taken care of that—Teachers' Association). The PTA is a national organization whose mission is to make every child's potential a reality by engaging and empowering families and communities to advocate for all children. So who do we blame? The answer is simple—all of us.

I noticed that Rosa was no longer speaking as a teacher; she was transforming herself into an advocate for her students and getting angrier. This was no longer about me writing a book; this was Rosa venting. She said, "There were some supplies, but they were not plentiful. You didn't have enough paper to hand out to students or workbooks to give to students to do their work in. If you had workbooks, the students couldn't write in the workbooks. They would use the workbooks but then give the workbooks back at the end of the class period so you could use them again with another class because you wouldn't have enough to go around, and even if you had enough to go around, you may not have enough for the next school year to use again."

Rosa was on a role. She also had some comments for them. As part of preparing future teachers for teaching positions, they did an internship. For many of them, they weren't placed in upscale schools. There was more frustration from Rosa: "I think all of us graduated from college with the idea of, 'I'm going to make a difference! I'm going in there, and I'm going to be the best teacher, and these kids, oh my god, they're going to love me, and I will change their worlds.' Well, it's usually the person teaching that gets the education and is using the person that's teaching whose world is changed, not the kids."

I thought that this was a good time to end the interview, but Rosa had years of frustration to vent, so I told myself, *I feel that you're doing these people a disservice because young teachers have no idea what they're walking into half the time, and that's why you have so many people leaving education and going into the corporate world.*

I heard Rosa and saw the change in her temperament when she spoke about her experiences. I asked her what would she do to change the system. It took her two seconds to get her thoughts together.

"First, I would promote from within; and when I say promote from within, I mean someone who has worked in the school and who has a good track record of teaching and working with students to the administrative positions instead of bringing someone in from the outside, or if I had to bring someone in from the outside, it would be someone who has an understanding and knowledge of the type of community that school is in. Not someone from Lincoln, Nebraska."

CHAPTER 14

Gaps in Unofficial Teacher Training

Rosa, trying hard not to discriminate, had a few things left to say, "These people from the suburbs can't learn how to teach in the hood." Because they can't. I've seen some wonderful teachers that live in the suburbs come into the inner-city schools and continue being wonderful teachers where the kids just love them to death. Rosa, ever the sensitive teacher now, had to make sure I understood correctly. Rosa continued, "Some of the kids love the suburban teacher and would follow them right up to Tarrytown if they had to." Then I would talk to some of these teachers and found myself saying, "Teaching here is really just not for you." They had no idea how to work with some of these students. New teachers would say to me, "What is your advice to me?" My advice back to them would be: "Don't show fear. Don't show fear; trust me under no circumstances should you ever show fear. Do you understand? Never show fear!" They would look at me like "What are you talking about?" I would say, "You will have some situations where kids will get right in your face, where they will stand toe to toe with you. Do not be the first one to blink. If they feel that they have scared you, if they had made you blink, if they have made you take a step back, then they feel, 'I don't respect you and I can do whatever I want to because I know you're scared of me.'"

For teachers that burn out or are incompetent, they have a holding room for the lack of a better term. I don't know why teachers are there—maybe for a disciplinary hearing or incompetence. They wait, and it takes the board of education forever to either do the hearing or make a decision. Until that time, they're not going to let you sit at home when they're still paying you, so they send you to maybe a district office or maybe to a school, and you sit in this classroom or this office all day long until hell freezes over. Then you go home, and you do this day in, day out, sometimes for the whole year or sometimes for two years until a decision is made. The students know. Talk about blinking.

Teachers know, and many are frustrated. I'll go into a closet and close the door, scream, cry, jump up and down, and say, "God, why am I here? I shouldn't be here." Then you can go to the bathroom and wash your face, comb your hair, and come back out as if nothing has happened, and you'll be all right.

Different than Pine Plains

CHAPTER 15

Gap in Rosa's Last Attempt

Rosa, ever sensitive and caring, said she would like to take some of these kids home or just give her whole paycheck to them and their family. To Rosa, they're just the sweetest, brightest kids, and her heart just hurts for them. One of the stories that she told me was about one of her physical education classes. She instructed her class, "Your tests for midterm will have a fitness course that you have to do, and at the end of the fitness course, you must be able to pull yourself up on the rope. Remember those ropes that would hang on the ceiling, and you had to climb up and down those ropes."

She explained to the class, "Not all the way up the ceiling, but you must be able to pull yourself up three times and then come back down. One, two, three, and then come back down. Remember what I said to you, 'I will not ask you to do anything that I cannot do myself.' I can't climb all the way up to the ceiling, so definitely not going to make you do it."

There was this young lady in the class—kind of heavyset—and she waited to be the last one to come up, and she couldn't get herself up. She couldn't even get her toes up off the floor. Of course, all the other kids laughed. That's something Rosa tried to stamp out in her classes. They do not make fun of anyone in there. They do not laugh at other people in there because if you laugh at someone because they can't do it one time, then that means you can come up there and do it ten times.

She felt bad, and of course, the kids giggled at her, and she couldn't get her toes up off the floor. Rosa said to her, "Listen, when do you have lunch?" She told her, and Rosa said, "Why don't you come and spend part of your lunch hour with me and we will work on this? I can help you. We'll work on this together."

She did, and Rosa was surprised but very happy that she came up every day, and they worked on strengthening exercises and worked on the rope and stuff. Every day, she would get better, and better, and better. On the day of the test, Rosa said to her, "When it's your time to come up, don't you dare hold your head down. You keep your head up, and you go and do what you have to do, and go sit back down. But don't you dare drop your head down." When it came time for her to do the test, she walked to the rope, and the kids were already sort of smirking. They thought, *We're going to get a good laugh.*

She walked up to the rope. She looked at Rosa and gave me a little smile; Rosa gave her a little smile, like, "You can do this." She was able to lift herself up three times and then work her way back down the rope.

She grabbed the rope and passed the test. You would have thought she was Miss America walking back across that floor to her seat. All the kids were just looking at her with their mouths open. They couldn't believe it. They didn't know what happened. She couldn't do this a few weeks ago, and now, "What happened?" Because they didn't know that they were working together. At the end of class, she waited for Rosa, and she said, "Miss Rosa, I just want to tell you how happy I am that you worked with me, and I thank you very much for what you did for me. I want you to know that not only this has helped me in my physical education class but also this has helped me in other parts of my life too. I have more confidence in myself now." Well, of course, the tears were just ready to start bawling like a baby, but Rosa was trying to keep the tears back and kept a smile on her face at the same time, and she gave her a big hug although they weren't supposed to hug the kids—she gave her a hug just like Rosa's seventh-grade teacher did to her and said, "I'm so happy for you, and I'm glad that I was able to help you. You have a good day now. Talk to you later." Rosa could tell from then on she did have a spring to her step, and you can see the confidence in her. What a big ripple into the community this was!

CHAPTER 16

Gap of School and Hood

Tanya is a teacher who leaves her comfortable home in the suburbs and commutes to the Bronx to teach in a title one low-income school where all the kids are from families of low income. When I first met her, I wondered, *How does this attractive, intelligent woman make it through the day in the hood?* I pictured Tanya as a fair damsel tied up and thrown into a lion's pit. It didn't take long for me to understand that she is strong and committed to helping children in the hood. Most of all, she understood that if you are teaching in a "foreign land," you have to learn the language and the culture and teach accordingly at different levels. Tanya has changed because she is now using a different lens to view life in the inner city. During the interview, she said almost apologetically or maybe it was a hint of embarrassment, "You understand that in the hood, I have a different persona." Put it all together, and you have a very remarkable teacher from the "burbs" who sends out wonderful ripples.

Tanya learned that the hood has more of a hold and draw on kids than the schools could ever have. One of the students at the high school was the shining star in the school. Everyone knew this kid was going places. He had the grades, and he had the personality—he had it all. Inside the school, he had everything going for him, and he had everybody pulling for him. Outside the school, it was a totally different story. And Tanya and I walked into the school one morning, and Tanya fully understood the power of the hood. There was a moment when she felt it was very necessary to say, "You know that when I am in the hood, I have a different persona in order to be more adaptable to the hood." When I went through my notes, I thought how wonderful that she felt it necessary to tell me that.

One morning, the power of the hood hit home. Everyone that Tanya ran into said, "Did you hear? Did you hear?" All she could say was, "Oh my god! Who got killed now? Who got arrested now? Who got into trouble?" They said, "Did you hear about Bobby?"

"Bobby? What about Bobby?" Everything seemed to be put fast-forward, and just to make sure you got the message, the same thing was said two or three times. Tanya tried to think good thoughts because it was Bobby. "Maybe he got a scholarship." These are good thoughts, and maybe the good thoughts will chase away any bad news. I mean, *What the hell are we talking about Bobby?* The good thoughts lasted for another two minutes, and for Tanya, it was reality. The star of the school had been arrested. Tanya was deeply saddened feebly protested, "Arrested? That can't be, not Bobby. No, are you sure? Arrested for what?" They said, "You remember that shooting when some gunmen went into this apartment, killed the family, and robbed the apartment stuff?" Tanya could see it coming. "Bobby was one of the gunmen." Tanya was numb, and her street education was almost complete. Tanya gave a feeble protest—it couldn't be him. Tanya was assured that it was Bobby, and Tanya tried to ease the pain by saying, "No, no, no." You cannot believe what people are saying to you. People are saying things to you. You're hearing it, but you can't believe it. Tanya could not believe that this had happened to this young man. It was two different lives. He had the life inside this school and then the life outside this school.

Inside this school, he was everyone's shining star. We just knew this kid was going places. We would not have been surprised that this kid had gotten a scholarship to Yale or Harvard or Princeton. That's how good he was. But then, on the outside, he was a totally different person within his neighborhood, and that's where the disconnect comes in at. Tanya was slowly coming back to the burbs and said that's where we need to figure out as a society how to bridge the gaps with these kids between home and school. It's just so frustrating and horrifying to think about why this young man had thrown his life away. All that had to do with probably his friends and family members because I found out too that sometimes it's not even friends that influence these kids to do things, but his family members—family members that encourage them to do things they shouldn't be doing. It's not all about killing and being arrested but family influence.

Planning for the future

Gap of Family and Pimp

One teacher told Tanya about one of her students. This young lady was dating a much older guy. I said to her, "Why is some mother allowing this to happen? What was this man in this girl's life? You know what I mean? This girl, she's a teenager, and this guy what? In his thirties? Forties? Are you kidding me?" I was told, well, her mother said to her, "Well, you wanted to date him, so date him. But if you break up with him, I'm going to beat your behind."

The mother's anxiety wasn't strictly about the daughter. These older guys give money to the household, and the mom doesn't want that money to disappear. As long as he wants you, you better be with him because he's helping to support this household. Now isn't that something? Talk about prostituting your children. My god, what do you say to this? I had nothing to say, but Tanya's education was now complete. Today she remains an outstanding teacher who doesn't mind crossing over the line to help kids in need.

Tanya told me about the parent-teacher conferences she had. One of her students' mom looked so young. I can't imagine how old she is. Her oldest son is in my class. He's ten. Then she has a little girl too. I thought that it was so interesting. I don't know how we got on the conversation, but I said that I had seen something posted online once. It was a mother's lament. It was something to the effect of "My home might be a mess, but instead of taking the time to make memories with my children, I clean." Tanya explained that she was not doing it justice at all to the lament, but it struck a nerve with the mother. The mother looked at me and said, "Wow. That's the exact opposite of the way that I run my life. Our kitchen floor—our apartment—has to be spotless."

Tanya shared more. "I thought that was interesting that my home is a mess (probably not) but hers is spotless. When I got home, I looked for an article about being White. I found an article, and the article said it has to do with class. Impoverished families want very much for their home to be spotless, to show that they are not as impoverished as their neighbors so it would be very important to them to keep their house clean. It tells the community that I may be poor, but I have not lost my dignity and respect like other people."

Tanya said, "You know, I was a little embarrassed because I had never thought of it that way. There's also a really interesting article, and I'll send you the link if you've never read it. It's called 'Unpacking the Invisible White Knapsack'."

The title does not even do it justice. You can read the article online. It's just all about these things that we don't think about. I grew up in the suburbs. I didn't know this at the time, but I wanted for nothing. You know, I had a lovely home, two working parents, a pool in the backyard, and people helping to take care of my brother and me. As much as I think, I know that article is so important; I think for educators in the inner city should read it.

Then this conversation with that mom the other day was really important. I'm not sure why she got very emotional. She's a young, young, young mom trying her very best for her little ones. I appreciated how raw and honest she could be even just getting choked up at a table. I said, "I get it. I'm a mom. We're doing the best we can. Use me. Let's work together." It's hard for her, and it will always be harder for her.

Two years ago, I had a student who grabbed a girl that he didn't know in the stairwell and tried to get her to kiss him. His mom worked double and triple shifts, some of which were mandatory. But while she was working so hard to provide for her family and keep her home clean, her son was falling apart without her. If she didn't work this hard, the chances were real that her whole family would be taken from her. So in addition to needing the money, we can put fear into the equation. I don't know how she lives from day to day.

CHAPTER 18

Gap of Basic Needs

Tanya asked me, "Norman, you mentioned that one of the complaints of kids in jail was the constant noise. Well, I think of that also in my students' lives—just the noise. They were put in contact with some agency associated with child services, and the woman would come into the home every week or every other week and give mom support in just basic homemaking and showed her where the food pantries were, helped her, and taught her how to keep the home clean." I don't remember what the religion was, but part of the religion was leaving out food offerings. And in the projects, when you have rats, mice, and roaches, that was really a problem for this family.

Just helping this family with those basics was wonderful. I had both girls and mom worked. They were Cuban. That was actually the only Cuban family I worked with. Just having that support was a relief for mom, but that was the only time I saw anything like that. Calling Child Services is not much of an answer either.

I have friends whose son is adopted and a child of color. Their son comes very often and comes over and plays with our daughter. Their grandson is Black. They are very White. They live right back there. Their daughter I think works for ACS. Yeah, she and I like to sit down every now and then with a bottle of wine. We just swap stories.

I don't know that there has been change. The more things change, the more they stay the same. I don't know what the answer is. I think it's just been so many years of more of the same, and so, I see many more years of more of the same.

With our inner cities just growing, I don't see an end. Unfortunately, even being as involved as I am, I'm not sure what the answer is beyond getting these resources for families that really need them. I think that each school should have… I mean my school is a pre-K to eight school. I think there should be guidance counselors and mental health services within the schools for all so that all of the families have access.

I think that until we do that until we really—in education, they talk about the whole child, and it's just words—look at the whole child and start helping families and meeting them where they're at. I think without that, it's just more of the same.

CHAPTER 19

Gap of Consequence

It's consequences for behaviors in the school with suspensions and detentions and all that, and in the cities, it's arrests and prison, but we're not getting to the root of the issues. It's being reactive instead of proactive.

Yeah, that's what I am in for. He stabbed one of my other former students over a stolen cellphone from a year prior. He wasn't even the aggressor in the situation. He's just the one that got the better of the other. The one who initiated the confrontation with two knives was never even arrested and questioned because he was almost killed.

Yeah. What do you think on a good day your biggest success is that you walk out, you get on the bus or the subway, and you say, "Yes, this was all right."

I just want my students to take responsibility for themselves, good and bad. I said, "You know me. I'm the kind of person who owns it. Whatever it is, just own it, take responsibility for it, and we're going to move on from there. Don't give me those, 'What did I do?' I can't stand those 'What did I do?' hands."

I have a different persona in Harlem, which I'm sure you figured out. Most recently, I figured out because my school is very competitive, and they're all about those test scores. They like to quote Maya Angelou when she said people will not remember what you said but they'll remember the way you treated them. Well, I believe my students are not going to remember their test scores in fifth grade, but they're going to remember the way Mrs. Oak treated them.

You know, my biggest success this week is parent/teacher conferences. I see one of my dad's friends coming down the hall—a big, black African man. I said, "Dad, come over here. Give me a hug." Then I said, "You're in the wrong hallway, though," because I know he's got two little girls.

His son, who is just my love, is in eighth grade, and he said, "No, I came to see you." He said, "Look at this report card." His son was not doing very well in eighth grade. He said, "Talk to him." "Okay, Dad."

I took a picture of the report card, and I immediately text messaged all of his teachers, "What can we do?" I just got an alert on my phone that tomorrow he gets his review sheet for science.

I spoke to all of his teachers, and I thought, *He'll always know that people are on his side. Just as you said, Norm, you hated high school, but a few years later now, you remember that teacher that looked you in the eye and treated you like a human being.*

Maybe it won't do anything now or tomorrow or next week, but I do feel like I'm planting the seed. I know that a lot of people think and sometimes even I think, *Am I making a difference? What am I doing?* Just banging my head against the wall. On my best days, I remember that I'm planting seeds.

CHAPTER 20

Gaps of Growth

I have known Michelle for a long time and was delighted when she agreed to be interviewed. We have connected at a whole bunch of levels about how to teach incarcerated children, and I have tremendous respect for her. Through the years, I could always count on her to be truthful and candid. In my book, she is my Rocky Balboa. True to form, Michelle didn't waste any time expressing her thoughts. I turned on the recorder and asked some questions, and Michelle was ready. I encourage the reader to stick with it because I have found that sometimes when talking to her it's like trying to take a sip of water from a fire hose, and that's high praise for my friend who sends out positive ripples.

"I'll first start by saying, when I was young and as a student, I struggled. I went through the public school system in one of the wealthiest towns in Westchester County, if not in all of America. It is well known for having wonderful resources. I was struggling since first grade. I was classified as a special education student and was also having some stuff going on at home. I will share that my father was incarcerated and that he was part of some of the trauma I was going through. I was having some emotional issues, and I was classified as having a learning disability in first grade."

Michelle shared, "As having been classified with a learning disability, I struggled through my whole entire education up through graduation. Had a lot of special education services, tutors, small classes, self-contained classes, big classes. I took some regents, and so I kind of knew I was going to go into education because I had some teachers that really impacted how I felt. This helped me to be more successful educationally. The problem was that it's not that I couldn't do it. I didn't know how and I didn't feel confident in trusting myself to want to learn and thought that I couldn't learn."

Michelle took a breath, and her spirit kept shining through. Like Rocky, she wasn't going to lose. Not surprisingly, she said, "I'm going to fast-forward a little bit. I barely made it out of high school, and I had to go to night school." When she said this, I thought, *No wonder I like her; she sounds like me in high school.*

I asked her, "Did those teachers influence your teaching career and show you how to teach that developed your way of doing things?"

"Yes. I think my very first skills teacher… I met with her one-on-one, and she did a lot of remediation with me in reading, writing, and math. She just made me feel very, very safe that it was okay for me to make mistakes. It was okay for me to ask questions. It was okay for me to just kind of say, 'I don't know.' She used multiple approaches until I learned. I was teachable, and I didn't think I was for a long time. It was very hard to explain when you're a child. You can't explain these things and you can't understand them. There were other teachers that their personalities were very warm. They were very fun and had a very fun class, and they engaged. They were very engaging with us. They also took the time to make it more personable. They'd bring in lunch for us, or they would take us out to lunch because we were such a small class. Our parents approved it and just made it more of a community type of feeling. There were of course a lot more teachers that did not make my education comfortable."

Michelle rolled on, "I later graduated. I did not go to college right away. I took time off because I hated school so much and I was so happy to be out of school. Prior to me graduating high school, I knew I wanted to work with students who had deficits and difficulties in school. I spent a summer in California. I worked at the neuropsychiatric institute. Excuse me, I volunteered, and this is when autism was in 1992. Autism was sort of like the new hot topic, the new buzz word. What is it? What does it look like? I did some work there, and then when I came back after that summer, I worked one-on-one with a girl who was autistic."

Gaps in the Desire to Be Better

I loved working with an autistic child. She was my parents' friend's neighbor, and so, I got to do some work with her. I also spent a lot of time in my early childhood babysitting. I loved kids, so fast-forward-ing again after high school, I stayed home. I worked; I tried some college classes to see if I could be successful. I was very bored and not challenged. After that, I visited friends at college, and I said, "Wow, you get to hang out and stay up late and look at all these people at parties and all these activities." Then I said, "I want this." I got into a college. It was in Boston, a small college outside of Boston, excuse me, in the suburbs and Newton, Massachusetts. I started going to some classes, and I said, "This is pretty easy." All you have to do is that you just have to walk in there, then they give you all these papers, and they tell you what you need to do. They tell you, "Oh, you're going to have this due on January 3."

I asked Michelle, "What was the magical turning point for you? Did you find a boyfriend?" Wisely, she skipped over that question and said, "Hey, lay it out for you. It's called a syllabus." I said, "Wow, this is going to work for me because now I know what to expect. I'm not walking in every day without an agenda or what's going happen." Having access to previewing what's going to come ahead was really beneficial for me. They had a resource center, and I'd go in there. The first time I went, the lady said, "Hi, I'm Vera. I'm going to be your tutor for the next year. Why don't you tell me how you like to do math or how you like to read?" Not surprisingly, my friend said, "If you talk to me like I'm a child, I'm going to cause a problem in here."

I wound up being on the honor roll in this college. I was taking like six or seven classes one semester and got on a roll, and I was like, "This is really not hard." I did well, and my self-confidence soared.

I have worked with Michelle for maybe four years with kids who are incarcerated. She's great, and there were times when I thought she was too hard on the kids. I remember a kid on his first day in lockup. Michelle said to him, "Why are you standing here?" He didn't know, but Michelle didn't put her arms around him to give a hug; she asked him what was he told to do. He remembered, and she looked at him and said, "Good." In one minute, she sent him a positive ripple and maintain discipline. Ever sensitive and caring, she could always be counted on to take care of kids with a need. She was also sensitive to adults. Once, when I went in for surgery, the first phone I received was from Michelle, "Hi, Norm. I'm concerned about you. Why did you have surgery? Are you okay? What's wrong?"

Michelle told me, "I moved back to New York, and I completed a bachelor's degree. That was where I did my associate's degree, actually in hotel restaurant management as well as some classes in education because I wasn't sure that I wanted to do the whole school thing after such a negative experience. But I came back to New York, went to college, Marymount College in Tarrytown, and got a dual degree in inclusive education, so I would be certified to teach regular ed and special education. Completed that program and got hired right after graduation. Graduated in December 2000 and began my first teaching experience in the South Bronx by Yankee Stadium at CES Community School, a community elementary school." This was on Sedgwick and the Highbridge projects; the housing projects were across the street from my building, so clearly, a lot of students came from there.

I was assigned to a special education classroom for students in grades three, four, and five. I had one paraprofessional with me in the classroom. I had an observation window, which was used on the other side by the school-based support team, so perhaps people that provided related services such as a psychologist, a social worker, and then speech pathologists would use that office for our kids or other kids. It was used for various reasons. The kids that I had here were very rough. These kids had very, very rough upbringings, and when I say the word rough, I mean difficult as in maybe weren't having meals. I had kids come in that had definitely suffered from some type of physical abuse. I had a kid come in with this shiner under his eye, and it wasn't "What happened, Jimmy? Did you fall down?" There was no real sense in talking about it; everybody in the school knew what happened.

CHAPTER 22

Gaps of Understanding

I had kids come in with razor blades under their tongues. These are third graders. Back then—I think going back twenty years ago roughly—this was a completely different generation. This was a different era. This was a time where even kids in the street had to be respectful to your neighbor if your adult neighbors said, "Stop," you had to listen. A lot of things have changed in terms of abuse and CPS, for valid reasons; we want to protect people and protect children, but I think there was some kind of OPed, if you will. They kind of overdosed a little bit on what they were doing because it really had an effect on the community. I had students that were not really receiving a lot of love and care at home, and I knew this because I had one student, David, who would not go home. Because he refused to go home, what he would do is that at the end of the day, he would sit on my foot and would curl his legs around my foot so I couldn't walk.

I'd have to lift my leg to actually move and call security; he just didn't want to go home. This was my very first class. I had about eight kids in there. They were maxed up to twelve. This was called a size-seven class or a miss two. These were the problematic kids. These were kids that were pushed out of even just regular special education classes and put into very small classes to have appropriate behavior management. Before school, I would have the students line up outside my door. I'd have them come in and then line up across the chalkboard. They'd have to say their name; they'd have to say good morning. You say, "Good morning. My name is Jimmy Jones.

I'm going to try my best to have a nice day." Then I'd have them empty their backpack just to make sure there wasn't any contraband or anything dangerous in their bags.

CHAPTER 23

Gaps of Shortage

"Michelle, at any point, did you have any of the supplies you needed, or was it always a problem?"

Quick to respond, she said, "No. No, there was definitely no supplies, and it was always a problem. I did have two computers, really old computers—two that worked. Then I had two that were just junk. They were stuffed in the back of this dumpy room that I really tried to brighten up. I had construction paper and the kids actually brought pencils to school. Textbooks, there weren't very many. Our kids sort of got short slighted, so I guess with that being said, special education students also got extremely slighted even more than everybody else."

"What did they do with the money? They didn't give it to you, where did it go? It's money and it's political. They're going to push the money wherever they're going to show that there's growth or wherever there's progress, and wherever the community complains that there are needs. I mean, let's be serious here. Let's be serious here. No, the government and the Federal government and New York State Education Department need to have data that's going to show that we're doing something with these kids. Right now, I think we have some really good people, the Board of Regents that are trying to do some really good things and that are trying to make these changes that are so badly needed.

"So your kids would suffer because they weren't progressing, not because it's any fault of yours. I think in schools everywhere, not just inner city, but more so within our city, the shift from when we were growing up really allowed a child or a student to explore their interests and their strengths. I don't think this era, this generation, this time that we're in is so focused on data and funding, and the political components to it trickle down to administration, trickle down to superintendents, trickle down to chairpersons, trickle down to all different types of administrators, district-wide on a district level, and then trickle into school buildings, which then trickle down to their staff, which then trickle down to these kids."

"It's a shame. It's a shame because their needs are so different and every kid in every school in every community is so different that it's hard to do a cookie cutter for everybody, for all the different communities and districts. But I feel like that's something that is a need. I think that one of the biggest components is that I won't just say some of these areas have gangs—some of them have guns. Some of these kids don't have money in their family, so they're out there hustling to put food on their table because all of this is relevant from many years ago. They did what they learned. Where do you think these kids ended up, your worst kids? Where do you think they ended up? They're out of school. Do you know what happens to the kids who we fail to help? A lot of them are in jail with you and me—a lot of them. I won't say all of them, but I know who they are. I worked in Arizona and worked in treatment centers. I've worked with sex offenders. I'm a licensed social worker. I've worked with lots of different types of people and lots of cultures, including Native Americans. I worked with kids who climbed over fences with no shoes on to get from Mexico into Arizona. Students aren't given the right tools. I don't think that it's really that much about supplies. I think it's really more about social emotional tools because if you can allow somebody to feel good about themselves—that it's okay to fail, it's okay to try it, it's okay to have an interest, and it's okay to like a girl if you're a girl—all these different things wouldn't happen. They're not educating a whole child, and they're not allowing for students to take on the interest and things that they're interested in. They're forced.

"There's a lot of schools that are student-centered—that are about students' strengths. They're about student growth. They allow a student to come in and say, 'Tell us what you like, and these are the classes you'll take.' They don't say you're going to take math, reading, writing, social studies, and science, and if you want, you can take a language. This is all a cookie cutter. America is a cookie cutter. America has one of the worst educational systems in the world. I mean, Norm, look at you. You turned out to be a wonderful success, and you had no intention of going to college, but different doors opened.

"They're not focusing on what's really happening in the real world, okay? Things change, and America's educational system is not changing with the world. You look at countries like China, for example. You look at different countries and how they operate and why it works for them. Why are so many people here struggling? Even people like me, I make just about six figures, and I struggle. I'm still paying off college loans and credit cards. It's not easy."

I said to Michelle. "You're in such a wonderful position to make assessments of where we are. I've known you for seven years, and I've always been impressed that you have a comprehension of the total picture. I mean, when you were talking to kids that were in jail, it was always compared to what's the big picture here, and you would focus on—I guess that you focused on—a child's needs, which make it student-centered, right? Did you bring that theory to jail?

"I think one hundred percent, and I think that's one of the benefits of being in the type of setting like that because you get to really focus on a child and what their needs are. In that type of setting, when we had twenty-four kids at the max, we had the time, and we had the ability to sit and talk about each child individually, and that's what they needed. We needed to know all areas of what was going on with them socially, emotionally, medically, and physically. You need to look at the whole child.

"Michelle, do you think suburban schools do that, or is it you who have to take Spanish or you have to take French or I forget who it was that I was talking to that? Oh, when starting out, they had a choice to take. In my grandchild's first year of high school, he has to take either Chinese, Arabic, or something else. I forgot what it was, but tough, tough languages; I think Mandarin, yeah.

"Now, she gets a lot of special attention because she's been tagged as she's just absolutely brilliant. I mean, she's carrying a 100.4 average. She's taken all these advanced placements That's wonderful, and that's going to set her up to get into a wonderful college. Don't forget a wonderful education, which is going to help her get a wonderful job."

Michelle said, "Does that translate to kids in the inner city, or is it just the lack of supply?" Well, I think it could translate.

Thoughts

CHAPTER 24

The Failure Gap

"Michelle, can you sum up what you have said so far?"

"I think I can." I also just shared that I'm not sure what the model that we use in—never mind the inner city—the whole country is. And with that, Michelle said, "Hold on. Let's take a break I'm getting into psych babble." It wasn't babble; she is very passionate about children's education, especially kids at risk. We talked for a while, and finally, I said, "Okay, let's go."

She said, "I'm always looking at a bigger picture, a macro level of what education really looks like. We're preparing them to go to high school and then to college or a vocational school and then go get a job. That's what we're preparing them for. We're not preparing them for life. We're not preparing them for trying to be well versed in different things.

"My friend's daughter is not being told, 'It's okay if you want to go ahead and sign up to learn about engineering. Why don't you come take a class in engineering? Why don't you come take a class in brain surgery?' She has many options. Others will never know what they can do. Who says that's the model that's going to work for every child? America has changed, but education has not."

Michelle was just warming up. "We're in a completely different generation, and so, the inner city just has it even worse than everybody else. They just have it even a thousand times worse than everybody else. They start from all the way in a dark hole, and they have to come out to see where everybody is now, while other people are advancing. I think not because they can't, not because they don't have that much access, but I think there could be a focus on other issues at that time.

"You could have a brilliant person come work for you at IBM that could make $400,000 a year and be an executive director. They could come from one of those projects, but because they don't have a degree, someone might not hire them. I think what I'm also saying is that sometimes, I'm not saying you don't need an education, but I'm saying you might not need social studies and algebra to get you to some of these places. Unfortunately, our society looks at you like that. You have to have a degree. If not, don't bother to apply."

That's why they write in job descriptions: this is what's required. That's what's required to do the job, but what's required for me to get hired? I could have experience. I might not have the degree, but I know I'm qualified. I said to her, "That would be printed black bold."

"What?"

"What you just said was a great statement."

"I don't know what I just said." God bless Michelle, always honest and straight forward.

Michelle is correct. I may not have a degree, but I know I can do the job that was advertised. When I applied for a job at IBM, I didn't have a degree, but in the preemployment test they gave, I knew I nailed it. During my interview at IBM, Mr. Bill Berry looked at the results of the test and my application, and I said, "I know I don't have a degree, but I'm asking that you give me a chance." We talked for about an hour, and a couple of weeks later, I received a job offer. I started in the supply room. I forget his exact words, but on my first day, Mr. Berry said, "You will be reporting to Mr. Pokorak." And I think he said or implied that I have my chance. Thanks to IBM's education program, I was able to get my bachelor's and master's degrees. Apart from my religious beliefs, everything I have I owe to IBM and Mr. Berry.

CHAPTER 25

Technology Brain Gap

I asked Michelle what she was doing now. She said, "Every student in my school has access to a Chromebook in every single class, okay? While every student has access to a Chromebook, they're learning how to use technology. They're getting a class all day long on how to use technology, but they already know how because they have phones. These kids have phones. They have iPads. They have video games. They know how to operate a machine. We're asking them to go ahead and write, type an essay, or do a blog. Here's a blackboard. There's one class that I work with, and we've post assignments up for them, and we tell them, 'You need to blog every night.' Instead of giving them a ditto, a worksheet, or a document, we say, 'Please go in and blog. Tell us your opinion. Tell us your thoughts,' creating higher-order thinking skills."

What this Chromebook does for them is that it gives them access to blogging. It gives them access to research, which is great, but they're not learning essential skills. They're not learning how to spell because the computer is doing it for them, and so, that's okay because maybe you don't need to know how to spell for the rest of your life because technology will take care of it for you. Even on our phones, it corrects it. It's helpful for learning technology, and that's really all it does, and it also assists some students that have difficulty with writing—kids that have struggles physically with writing. They can use a typewriter. Kids who have communication disorders maybe can use technology to help them communicate. Do they have access to Siri and Rosa? My wife always says that's ruining a kid's brain because they don't think out an answer; they ask Siri and Alexa, or they just say Google. It's almost the same, just Googling is kind of the same as Siri. That's where I think Siri and Alexa get their information from.

I don't know. It can be really helpful technology because they can find information. I'm not really sure whether you even need the skill anymore to go to a dictionary. I don't remember the last time I picked one up. If I needed it, I would use my phone. I told Michelle, "It's funny how every day *Merriam-Webster Dictionary* gives me the word of the day, and I'm addicted to it, which is great."

We had talked really briefly for a minute about individual plans, so to speak, about the kids in jail, how we were able to really individually diagnose strengths and deficiencies or deficits for kids, barriers, and things like that. However, because they weren't there long enough—some of them weren't, but most of them were—you couldn't really get a whole child. What does that look like for a child? What do they need socially? What do they need educationally? They might not need to know about Tecumseh, but they might need to know where New Mexico is on a map. How do you figure out what that looks like for each kid? I don't know. The inner-city kids have the same access to quality education. I think because in New York City specifically, there are some really wonderful schools, of course, New York City public schools, but there are also some really crappy schools where they need bodies. It speaks volumes when you look at how infrequently they refuse to shut schools down when there is very hazardous, increment, dangerous weather going on.

CHAPTER 26

The Why Not Gap

They won't even close down a school because as people say, it's a babysitting service. That's why they don't close the schools—too much money lost. Nobody knows where to put the kids. Every kid should have an individual plan, especially kids in the inner city because they have so much access to different schools and different programs, but they don't utilize them. In my opinion, they don't utilize them the way they could, and it would take a lot of work to kind of revamp the whole educational system in our country. Never mind New York, but just what that whole picture looks like. I think New York could be a great place to do it. There are lots of access, lots of things, and lots of people willing to help create that. People like yourself who just go out and say, "I want to go do something. How can I change? How can I impact? How can I keep learning? How can I try to make sense of some of these things?" The current climate and environment also speak a lot. With technology, with access to so many things in the inner city, you can have anything at the fingertips that you want. From bacon, egg, and cheese to a pack of cigarettes to drugs, you can have anything.

"How about guns? Was that ever a problem in school?"

"In my schools? Yeah. I asked the question this morning. Why do all these mass shootings in schools appear to happen in suburban, White-dominated schools but never in the inner city ever?"

They're happening. They happen every day. They're just not reported.

That's right. They're usually just onesies or twosomes, right? It's just that one person gets shot or two get shot, but I never read seventeen, twenty, or twenty-five kids were just shot in the South Bronx. I never, never read about this, or never has it become so common in the inner city; we don't even bother reporting half of them.

There was a newer shot recently. In the past few months, there were some stabbings, and there was some violence. The city went into an uproar because after the first one, that was enough, but then it happened again. Then I believe it happened again, and the community was in an uproar, but what is the reason that this community got in an uproar? Why, really? Why isn't it Yonkers? Why isn't Yonkers or Mount Vernon in uproars, when this is part of their daily schedule? This is what happens every day there, in some areas, and there are people and activists who are trying to make a change, but this was in an area that is not recognized as an area where there's a lot of violence or drugs and access to these things and is also a diverse community.

You have a north end, you have a south end, and that's why the community was in such an uproar. You don't see that everywhere. Who do we point the finger at? Is it the schools? Is it the parents? Is it the kid? No, it's the culture, and it's the environment. That's what it is. You can't blame a parent. Everybody says the parents, but what were they doing? The parent was probably at work, or the parent wasn't even aware, and you can't hold a parent accountable for that. That's ridiculous. A lot of these parents that I've seen come crying, begging for help. What do I do? They go to the police, and they report their own kids because they don't want to get in trouble and they want help. That's kind of what I mean when I say the current climate and environment.

What do you see as the future for Michelle? For me? Yeah, oh god, education or not education, is there anything? Ten years from now, I'm going to call you up and say let's have lunch.

CHAPTER 27

The Plan

Michelle explained, "I have a lot of ideas and I think I'm currently struggling with what I want to do, where I want to do it, and how I want to do it because it's sort of a mix of 'I have to stay with working with at-risk kids,' and when I say at risk, I mean behavioral, I mean financial, I mean emotional, and I mean the whole package. The only places you can really do that are in schools, residential settings, jails, after-school programs, or therapeutically. I'm not really sure, and I'm kind of... I don't know. I mentioned earlier that I'm going to be getting involved in a community center. I don't know how, or I'm not sure how. I do want to leave a trademark.

"I do want to leave my mark somewhere. I just don't know how, and I want to be a part of something. I'm not sure what that is, but perhaps, when it comes my way, I'll know. This is really just modern-day chaos; it is what it is. You're still recording? I have more things to say. You still recording?"

"Yup. I'm still recording and I also wanted to say something."

"I want us to speak a little bit more."

"It's okay. I want to speak briefly about how culturally—and I don't mean ethnic cultures, but I mean environmental culture norms—they're acceptable. We accept everything that's going on around us.

"Really? Really, how so?"

"See, now, I'm in a psychobabble mode. It's now psychobabble time. We walk around the streets, and we see crap all over the place. Do we stop and pick it up?"

"In Japan, what do they do? Do they allow that? That doesn't happen. Everybody has a respectful community. People respect one another. They respect their environment. They respect their people. They respect their culture. Okay. That's one example. How so? In my school building, why don't we respect our culture? Why do you think?"

"We haven't been exposed. We don't know what that looks like. You don't know what that looks like. I watch, I've sat, and I've observed. In my building, I've watched administrators walk around, and I see water bottles in the hallways. You think they'd stop and pick it up? They don't, and I'm not speaking to the current building I'm in; I'm speaking in different buildings. I like to sit back and kind of watch. I like to observe. I like to see what's going on. These are people that are supposed to be role models. That's acceptable. It's acceptable to have bubble gum on your walls in a school building. It's acceptable to have kids running around cursing. It's not okay, but it's acceptable. There's a very big movement right now with restorative justice and restorative approaches. There is a school in the Bronx I know where they only practice restorative justice and restorative approaches."

"They only practice what?"

"Restorative. That's the only model they use in their building. Whatever kids are doing, when they are committing offenses that are a disciplinary action based on whatever handbook and whatever it is through the district codes and stuff like that, they've decided to go another route with it. The model allows students to learn from their mistakes and what they could do differently. I don't care how many mistakes kids make. They have to learn, so our educational models, most of them, teach discipline. This is your consequence. Your parents teach it. If you come home late, you're going to get grounded. If you got a bad grade in school, I'm going to take your video game away. That approach in school carries. It's a home and school thing also—the whole, it takes a village. You got to have a partnership at home and in school."

There is fun

CHAPTER 28

Watching the Kids Gap

Some of these parents aren't home in the inner cities. There's my babble again, but it's coming back to the inner cities. Instead of teaching them, I can't have you out late. It's scary; it's dangerous. I worry; I physically worry about you when you're not home. Can you please call me if you're going to do this again? Please understand that it hurts me. That's not what's being done in schools. They look for suspensions. A lot of schools look: "I'm going to suspend you. You're going to the principal's office. How would you like it if I called your mother?" They use threats: "Stay after school; I'm giving you detention." Everything's a punishment. It's not learning. That's not learning. The school I'm thinking of in the Bronx told the person I know that was a dean there. He gave me one experience, and I thought… He shared an experience that I thought was really great: he had a bunch of kids he took on a class trip.

It was overnight. One of the kids brought some alcohol; they got drunk. There was a problem of some kind, and they could have suspended them. They could have expelled them, and this was a New York City public school that sort of used a different approach in their school. They wanted to go a different route. They didn't want to use the disciplinary codes of New York City. What they did was that they told all these kids that got caught drinking, "We'd like you to go to a drug and alcohol class and attend it." I don't know if it was two classes, four classes, or one class or how many hours, but they were required to come back and report to everybody who was on the trip that night and tell them what they learned from the class about drugs and alcohol and how it could affect them and what they learned from it. What they learned from these kids was that they learned to build rapport with these kids, as the adults. They also learned about their strengths, and so they pulled from that, and they learned that a lot of these kids were very talented artistically.

These kids then created a mural for the school that went upright when you walked in the building. They applauded their talents, and they learned at the same time. The parents obviously were made aware of everything, but they just used a different approach. It was also this building that uses a very student-centered approach, so they don't rely on adults to make decisions. They use a council of students to do that. Something I learned at the jail from one of the directors was that there was a model that was used that was called a sanctuary model. No, I'm sorry, scratch that. I think it's called the Missouri model. The Missouri model is used in juvenile justice. In Missouri, they used it where the children were the ones doing restraints on other children. They didn't allow adults to touch kids. It was the students or the kids doing it, so it was kid-based. Right now, in New York state, there's a push to allow students to run their IEP meetings: their special education and their Individual Education Plan (IEP).

There's a push for them to start doing that. Nobody's doing it. There are maybe a few states that are doing it, but it's really not happening. Is it good to use it?

I think it could be very beneficial. However, you could be facing a lot of lawsuits that happened because of noncompliance and things that aren't being done as per the IEP, so it could be hard.

CHAPTER 29

Success

Myrlie started her own business fifteen years ago, and when she looks look back at her path, she often thinks about her journey. She is actually thankful for growing up the way that I did. She grew up in the city in the projects in the South Bronx. Myrlie said, "I knew all the local drug dealers. They would throw cookouts in the summertime for the kids, and you know, when you're young, we really didn't look at them as the bad guys. We looked at them as someone in the community who threw great summer block parties for kids. But now as an adult, I'm like, "Yikes! What was I thinking?"

Myrlie explained, "But that is the way it was. 'You don't know what you don't know.' When I think of my story, I was having a strong mother. My father was definitely in my life, but my parents were divorced, so I lived with my mother. My mother always worked and always made sure that I went to school, made sure that I had breakfast, and made sure that I did my homework at night. I was a typical teenager. Going out, I was going to clubs at fifteen. I think of that too. I look at my daughters, and I'm like, 'Oh my gosh. I can't believe that I was going to the clubs at fifteen years old.' But I was a city girl. That's kind of what we did."

Then Myrlie became reflective and said, "But it was different. I do have friends who I grew up with who were the same age as me, and their path is very different. I have friends through Facebook who still connect with people that I grew up with, and you see people who you last saw when you were twelve or fifteen years old. And I know of some friends who were strung out on crack and who had kids really early and now at this age are grandmothers, like multiple grandmothers that are in my age group. Just really a different path."

I think of some of the people who were having a rough time, didn't have parents around, or had a mother who was also on drugs. So I know for a fact that that makes a difference in your life no matter where you live."

When you're going to school, you don't know what you don't know, right? This is a true story. I'm not gonna say what school because I don't want this to get published and then they come after me and try to sue me. But this is an actual story that you're gonna find unbelievable.

When we first moved to the projects, I went to an elementary school that was pretty close to the project where we lived. I didn't like the school, and I told my mother, "I don't like the school." Kids are kids. But in regard to the teacher, I just didn't like the teacher. He just really wouldn't teach. I remember one day in school. This is a true story, and it's unbelievable. He was reading the newspaper and smoking a cigarette. You think about it back then. Now you can't smoke cigarettes anywhere; you couldn't smoke cigarettes I'm sure in school. But he was smoking cigarettes at his desk reading a *New York Post* or *Daily News* or one of those kinds of newspapers. As a young child, I was just like, "This is crazy. I don't think he's supposed to be doing this in school," like we were talking and doing what we were doing. And he was reading a paper and smoking a cigarette in the classroom in the South Bronx. So I went home, and I told my mother. I was like, "Mom, I don't believe this or accept it" and she says, "That can't be." And I said again, "It's true. It happened." And my mother obviously went to the school, and they were like, "Well, this is your neighborhood school, and this is where she needs to stay." And my mother was like, "You need to make arrangements to get her to another school, or I'm going to report that this is what the teacher was doing." And they allowed me to go to another school.

CHAPTER 30

Gap of Believe

So I think of that story, and I tell my daughters, and they're like, "Oh my gosh." That could never happen in Westchester county. You know, the fact that that even happened in the South Bronx is unbelievable.

So there are disparities, of course. It's different. I compare my education to my children's 'cause that's what I'm the closest to. Do you know what I mean? For me, all of my friends went to the area schools, so I can't say what someone in Westchester who was my age or what it was like back then because that was all that I knew. Now, as an adult, I look at my children's experiences, and I see like, "Oh my gosh. This is just like night and day." So it was different. But I think again what saved me was that I had a mother who made sure that I did my homework—who made sure that I did everything that I had to do. It's not the same. And if you don't have anyone in your corner kind of guiding you, I feel like that's what makes the difference.

I moved out of the South Bronx when I was an adult. My mother still lives in the South Bronx. I mean it's by choice. She's comfortable. That's where she lived, and she's happy there. I knew that I didn't want to live there. Once I got married, I didn't want to have children to grow up in the projects, and I didn't want stay in the South Bronx. I mean I still go to the Bronx, and I still have friends that are there, and my mother is still there. But I just wanted something different for my kids.

My husband grew up in the South Bronx. We both grew up in the same projects. So it's the same thing for him. It was just like we wanted something different. Plus I think one of the things too is exposure, right? So for me, I had my first internship when I was in high school, when I was at Booz Allen Hamilton, 101 Park Avenue. So this is a young lady who grew up in the projects in the South Bronx, and I had my first internship at a huge corporation right in midtown Manhattan. I remember office parties and it's funny that I'm an event planner now, right? But I remember office parties; going to the holiday party was at the Guggenheim. I remember this from being—what was I—sixteen or seventeen.

I was just like, "Wow, this is nice. This is different. This is how people live? This is how people celebrate? It's very different from what you see growing up in the hood, growing up in Patterson projects." The same thing with my husband. My husband interned at Cushman and Wakefield—the big real estate firm. So he often talks about how they would go to the Hamptons for his holiday party and he was just like, "This is amazing. This is how people live?"

So I think for us, having that exposure piece really makes you say, "I don't wanna stay here because there's all of this stuff happening. I wanna do some of this." So I think it's kind of a combination. One thing is that I had a strong mother in my life. With my husband, it is the same story. He's successful in his own right.

CHAPTER 31

Outlook: Over the Gap

My husband had a strong mother, right? And then I think it's the parenting, making sure that even though your schools are not as great, you do everything that you need to do to survive to go to the next level. I think that is definitely a solid piece.

It's just the value of working. My first job was at Burger King when I was fifteen years old. That was something very important for my mother—to teach me the value of working. And it's the same with my husband, in working and in interning, being exposed to things that are outside of your neighborhood so you're not in the South Bronx. You're seeing how other people live, how other people celebrate, and how other people do things. I think that kinda brightens your horizons and makes you wanna get out of that situation.

And then I feel like some of the people that have gone a different route that grew up in the South Bronx didn't have a strong mother as I mentioned. And they a lot of times didn't leave the neighborhood. You know, they might not have had a job in Manhattan or somewhere else or never got on a plane and went anywhere so they weren't exposed to other things. So I think it's kinda like a pie, and I think these are all pieces of the pie. So I feel like if you stay there and you don't have anyone in your corner, you're gonna get in trouble. Chances are that you're gonna get in trouble. And you don't know what you don't know. So if you never leave the neighborhood, you don't know what else is out there.

You'd be surprised how people grow up in the South Bronx, which is so close to Manhattan, but never venture out.

What about the view of the police? That has changed so dramatically that I can't believe half of what I hear.

And I see the first couple of shootings of kids of color, and you're kinda sitting there saying, "Well, obviously something's wrong." And then pretty soon, you start to turn and you start to think, "What the hell are we doing?

I need you to really be very clear when you write about this 'cause I don't want my words misconstrued. So police brutality in areas of color is a thing. It's not imaginary. It's something that… These are conversations as Black parents, and these are even conversations even living up here that I have with my children. Every Black friend that I know that has children, especially boys, knows that you must have a conversation with your children about how to interact with police because it's a reality.

I don't have any ill will toward the police. God forbid if there's a situation, I'm happy to see a police officer. In my business, I interact with police officers all the time working on huge festivals and keeping everyone safe and having meetings with the police chief. I value what they do, and I appreciate what they do.

And it's something that people—not of people that are of color—sometimes wonder about, "Well, is it really a thing?" It's a thing. It's something that you have to talk to your children about. I remember I went to my mother's house. I drove a BMW, and it was a bad snowstorm, and I was double-parked because of course, the snowplow that comes around up in Westchester keeps our streets nice and clean. In South Bronx, the snowplow I guess doesn't make it on those blocks.

So it was literally snow, no walkways, so I was double-parked in the street; and a police officer came down, and he spoke to me. My husband ran upstairs; my daughter was in the car. He came, and he's like, "What are you doing here in this car?" He just spoke to me so nastily and so like I wasn't a person. And I kinda got into words, "'cause, Amy, you know me very well. You know that I just am sweet (big smile) and I'm kind, but I'm not just gonna let you talk to me any kind of way. Like you know that about me."

So we got into some words, and it was just... I was lucky because I probably shouldn't have given him back mouth or sass. But he was so disrespectful, and I said to myself, *Had I been a White woman sitting in this car or had I been in Westchester sitting in this car.* I just couldn't even imagine that same scenario that happened in the South Bronx—the way he spoke to me with my daughter in the car, like I was—excuse my French—a piece of shit. I could not imagine that happening in Westchester, and it was very upsetting. Even my daughter was in the back like, "Oh my god. We didn't even do anything. Why is he talking to us that way?"

Reality Gap

As a Black person, you're like, "Oh my gosh." Yeah, I mean it's a reality, and unfortunately, I hope that one day it won't be, but right now, it is. Yes and here you are. And here I am. From flipping burgers and being exposed to other upscale events, Myrlie was driven to leave the South Bronx for the most basic reasons. I want some of that and she did so by hard work, honesty, and integrity.

Yeah, in some ways, it's kind of a hopeless environment. And I say this. I don't feel like I had a horrible childhood. I can't even tell you I had a horrible childhood. I had a great childhood growing up. I remember us playing in the water fountains and things that you see on television and having a good time. I had a great childhood. But just as a young adult, I just knew that I wanted more for my children.

That was really it. It wasn't… I think I'm a determined individual, and I think that I would have succeeded really anywhere. But it was just more of a preference. I just wanted a different life for my kids. A piece of that too was when I was in probably about eleventh grade; I went to go live with my grandmother for about a year and a half. I was having trouble in school, and my mother wanted to send—you know, that was like the boot camp—me to my grandmother who's very loving.

But anyway, long story short, I went to live with my grandmother for a couple of years and in South Carolina. Yeah, South Carolina. So that was very different because I went to a school that was majorly White. My school was in the city. We didn't have a lot of

White kids in our school. It was a city school, and there were really not a lot of White kids in our school. There were very few.

Yeah. So that was a shift for me when I went to South Carolina when I went to school. I remembered too that this is having never really been in class with White students. I wondered when I walked in, *Look at all these students. It's a majority of White students.*

In my new school in South Carolina, there were a few Black kids—maybe four or five. And I remember feeling vulnerable like I never went to school with White kids. I thought, *Are they smarter than us? Are they this? Are they that?*

I think back now, and I'm like, "How silly." But you don't know what you don't know. So I think a piece of that too was a reason for me wanting to have my children live somewhere where it was very diverse and was different from my experience. However, I still take my kids down 'cause I want them to know about that part. Because that's a part of me. And I want my kids to be street smart. And sometimes, living up in the suburbs, there are certain things where you just… My husband and I joke about things that our daughters do, and we're like, "Picture that in the projects."

"Myrlie, are you like your mother?"

"I think I am very much like my mother. My mother says I have more drive, and sometimes she's like, 'Oh, sit down. Just relax.' You know? So I think I get that keep going from my father. But I do think I'm a lot like my mother. My mother's very strong, very loving at the same time, very caring, but no nonsense. So I do feel like a lot of my qualities I get from my mom."

Yeah, kids are kids. My middle school, I remember, was right across the street from my house, and we had a great principal. Also, we had a wonderful dean; I remember him. They kept us positive, and they were men of color. They kept us on task. I really thank God for I had good childhood memories. I know that we didn't have everything that other kids had, but we had enough.

Another funny story that I tell my kids now that I remember is that *The Brady Bunch* was like one of my favorite shows. I love *The Brady Bunch.* You know how the kids had the bathroom, the Jack and Jill that would open on both sides and there's a staircase that kinda went down? I remember talking to a friend, and they said something about their house, "Look at that bathroom. I would love a bathroom like that." And I'm like, "That's not real. Nobody lives like that. That's TV." I thought that was kinda like a set—like a TV set. I didn't think that people really had homes like that. Growing up, I thought everybody lived the way I lived.

CHAPTER 33

Gap of Misinformation

Misinformation and made-up stories are one of the biggest problems society faces. Social media exasperates and makes it extremely hard to determine what is the truth. When dealing with kids who are incarcerated, you have to be careful not to get sucked into some story where they are the victim. It's important to correct them in a way that won't embarrass them.

One kid was telling me how awful the cops were. He explained that once when he was walking down the street, a cop car pulled up and the cop picked him up, slammed him down on the sidewalk, then picked him up, threw him against the cop's car, picked him up, put handcuffs on him, and threw him into the back seat, and slammed the door shut.

So I said, "Wow that's quite a story, but I want to make sure that I heard everything correctly. You were walking down the street whistling a happy tune." He told me, "No, I wasn't whistling."

"Okay, you didn't do anything. You weren't giving him any sass, and boom, without any warning, he starts pushing you around." He conceded that he may have said something, but he didn't remember. "So he picked you up. I mean you are a big guy and he must have been a very strong police officer. How high, up to his shoulders? It might have been up to his waist?" I was starting to smile. Maybe he pushed me. "I mean you know these things happen quickly. And the possibility exists that you are playing me." He started to smile and sat down secure in the knowledge that the class understood that he was just playing around. He wasn't embarrassed—no harm, no foul.

Sometimes, there is no playing around as Billy told me that he and his friends were walking along and just grab-assing around. A cop came up to them and asked, "What's going on?" Billy added, "I told him that we were just playing around. So he took my cigarettes out of my pocket and tore off all the filters and stomped on the cigarettes and said, 'I just saved your life.' I was trying to tell him that I paid for them and he didn't have any right to do that, and then I kept my mouth shut. Do you think he had any right to do that?"

From the look on Billy's face and the sad look in his eyes, he was being truthful, and I said, "No, he did not have the right to do that." Hard to say definitively, but Billy looked genuinely pleased that someone believed him.

Sammy told me about the time he and his friends were in a burger place and they started playing around, "I slipped, and my gun fell on the floor. The manager went all ape shit on us and called the police. We just ran out the side door." I said, "I can see how you would be annoyed with the manager freaked out, a bunch of kids come in, and one or two has a gun." That was an awful thing he did. It was a nice try, but I see a few holes in that story. I loved his response, "Yeah, okay, but hey, yo, you know right? Translation, that does happen, but I wanted to put a show on the for the class."

Sanchez looked upset. It was about four weeks after Trump got elected, and he was scared. He said that now the government was going to pick him and his family up and send him back to Mexico. I said, "You and your family are Americans. Why would they do that?" He said, "I don't know. I hear people talking."

There is terrible and hurtful information from social media and crazy political promises. I used Shana's letter in my talks and emails. Shana's letter should scare parents.

Shana wrote as follows:

> "I first entered the system when I was fifteen years old, but my troubles started far earlier than that. I grew up in a wonderful community with my mother and father and had what almost any child would want. I was a high honors student

and competed in sports throughout my childhood. Although deep down, I was never entirely
happy. By twelve years old, I was getting drunk
with the older kids, and at fourteen, I was beginning my use of hard drugs. It was all an experi-
ment at first…testing my limits to see how much
I could handle. By fifteen years old, I knew I was
a full-blown addict. Pills, coke, weed, dust, and
anything that I could get my hands on would
satisfy my growing addiction. My friends and
family tried to help, but there was only so much
they could do. I was stealing from everyone and
anyone just so I could supply myself with my
next fix. Eventually, this behavior caught up to
me, and I was arrested for robbery. By now, I
had found my drug of choice and the one that I
would be struggling to detain to this very day—
heroin. I am now seventeen years old. Since my
first arrest two years ago, the system has put me
through various treatment programs, all of which
I failed because my addiction took hold of me.
I ran away from every single one, plummeting
even deeper into my hole than before I started
putting myself in positions that I never thought I
would ever have to go through. It took me until
March 30 this year, when I was remanded to jail,
that I seriously need to get my life together. I will
be doing the remainder of my time in a limited
secure facility where after two and a half years, I'll
finally be released. I was able to obtain my GED
while being in one of the rehabs, which proves
that anything is possible for anyone! It took a lot
for me to learn my lesson and really start taking my life seriously. My addiction could be an
example to kids my age; you never have to take
it to the point that it wants you to. If you let it,

it will take over everything you are—mind, body, and soul. Kids like us always have the opportunity of a second chance—never forget that!"

A number of kids who are incarcerated will tell you that marijuana is the gateway to all drugs. Today in our society sacrifices our society by simply saying, "marijuana is a recreational drug." This lie has worked its way into our lexicon. All for the sake of adding more money to states treasuries and we don't mind sacrificing our kids. We should all hang our heads in shame.

CHAPTER 34

Recognizing a Gap

Sometimes the problem of shrinking the gap looks simple. So what is the plan for the future? It is fairly simple: education and more education and making sure that people in the inner city have access to what they need for a healthy and bright future. On the surface, it should be easy to identify the problem areas. New York City has a population of 8,622,698, and 26,188 live in each square mile. In Pine Plains, they have a population of 1,353, and 83 live in each square mile. To accommodate a growing population, NYC expands by going straight up with their buildings. Surrounded by bridges and water, NYC can only accommodate a growing population by going north and northeast. It was unthinkable in the '60s and '70s that a two-hour commute is okay. Pine Plains stays the same except for the fact that people from the city are buying up land, and it's fair to say that the face of Pine Plains is changing. During one of my trips to Pine Plains, I almost ran off the road when I realized one of the most beautiful farm areas had been converted to a Polo field. I decided not to research how that happened, but I can only imagine that area farmers gagged at the view.

Based on an article in Wikipedia, the local farmers are pushing back with sarcasm and cynicism. Forty years ago, the founder of Carvel Ice Cream was the first to try to convert the land into a second-home golfing community. He built a Golf Hall of Fame, invited friends George Steinbrenner and Perry Como to play on weekends, and designed one hole to resemble his Fudgie the Whale ice-cream cake.

"I thought people with money would flock from the city," says Charles O'Donnell, then the attorney for Mr. Carvel, who died in 1990. "It just never got off the ground."

But Mr. Carvel couldn't win over the local farmers who still mockingly recall his New York adviser who paraded around in a blazer monogrammed with his family's "royal crest" and called himself "the count." Mr. Carvel abandoned the project after selling seventeen homes. His vision of a tribute to golfers is a small concrete building, condemned because of a large crack in one wall. Today, according to the latest post in Wikipedia, Manhattan skyscraper developer Douglas Durst hopes he has better luck than ice-cream pioneer Tom Carvel on this same bucolic site in the shadow of the Catskill Mountains.

I understand that today the Durst Foundation is trying again. The foundation who has developed office towers around Times Square and Grand Central Station wants to build 951 homes on the former Carvel property and surrounding farms. That's less than half of the houses planned forty years ago. Hoping his project will avoid the fate of the late Carvel, the Durst Foundation had pledged an environmentally friendly development that includes corridors for passing wildlife and recycled water for the twenty-seven-hole golf course.

I'm sure that Messrs. Carvel and Durst are fine people, and while all this is going on, kids in the inner cities are watching the beginning of a big exodus from the city to the north. These are the kids who are waiting for their chance to a piece of the American dream. Chances are if you are a child of color in the inner city, you probably won't get it. But somewhere in the distant suburbs, the majority of people are rejoicing that they have succeeded and have reached the American dream plateau. No doubt they worked hard to get there and deserve the fruits of their labor. But for every success, there are kids being denied a good education because their teachers can't get proper supplies or have simply been overwhelmed by their environment.

CHAPTER 35

Bridges

Fixing the problem of poor education in the inner city has been going on for years, and it seems an attitude of "What the hell is the sense of trying" to have set in. It can be fixed.

Bishop Paul Moore once told me, "You can't teach Christianity to a hungry person; first, you have to feed them." On the same level, you can't feed a child's brain unless you have quality schools and supplies. There are successes in the inner city because of exceptional families who refuse to admit defeat and give in to political inaction and a negative environment. We can change things around, but it will take hard work, *respect for all people,* and honesty. Nothing will be changed by cutesy politically correct expressions and phony platitudes.

The first step will be to make presentations to corporate America. For example, Metropolitan Insurance spent $400 million payable over twenty years for the naming rights to the new Jets/Giants football stadium. It is now called MetLife Stadium. With exception of some shows, it sits empty after the football season. I just gave up my season tickets to the Jets, and the name of the stadium never meant a thing to me—zero, zip, nada. But it would have been very impressive if I drove by a school and saw that MetLife won the naming rights for a rundown school. Citibank won the naming rights to Shea stadium for $400 million payable over twenty-five years and $17 million or $18 million per year. Does anyone think that the NFL and MLB need the money more than a school for kids? And while we are at it, push the envelope a little further, tax support only for naming rights to a school. The money would go directly to the school with a professional auditor on the premises to keep track of the money.

Imagine if you saw the name Merrill Lynch on a school, you would know immediately that it was with an accent on family finances and investing for the future and a very special school. I introduced the stock market to kids in jail, and they can't wait to see the results of their investments. How about Tesla at a school? And you knew immediately that school was about electronics and car design or Anderson Windows for trade and design. How about Kohler for plumbing, or Architect, Engineering, Consulting, Operations and Maintenance (AECOM) Technology Corporation, or General Motors for mechanics? The garage down the street has had a sign up for a year "mechanic wanted" and can't fill the position. High school is not all about preparing kids for college; it's about preparing them for life, and there are a lot of tradespeople who make a very good living driving trucks and fixing things. Magnet schools have taken a step by having schools specialize in a certain career discipline, but think of the educational explosion in the inner city when Corporate America starts to hang signs on schools and a corporation like NIKE starts teaching sports-related classes. I would dare say the absentee rate would cut to five percent.

While this is happening, I don't expect the parents to be idly standing by. They can give either time, talent, or money, but when they do, put their name on a plaque and start hanging them all over the school. It will create an enormous sense of pride that their family improved education in their area.

A wonderful friend, each year, gathers people together, solicits school supplies, and puts them all into backpacks for kids who need help. This year, Susan (she is one of the people I dedicated my first book to) and her team distributed two thousand backpacks filled with needed school supplies. This is a wonderful accomplishment. Now what is needed is for Corporate America to build on Susan's success. Go through a school and make a list of what is needed: Do rooms need painting? Is the heating system okay? Is the roof leaking? Overall, is the building in good shape? Find out from the teachers what they need. My friend, leadership guru Alisa would be perfect for this. Leadership and her was a match made in heaven.

I'm a retired IBMer, and a nonprofit wrote to IBM asking if they would lend them an executive to help them set up the first HIV/AIDS center for families impacted by this disease. They agreed, and I was chosen. I was there for sixteen months. From personal experience, I know that having a corporate name attached to an organization helps. Imagine what it would mean to a school knowing that they were attached to Chase, Netflix, or Amazon.

Before I left to return to IBM, I met with a number of large companies and politicians explaining some of the challenges we faced.

One meeting I remember was a presentation to the late Congressman Hamilton Fish. I mentioned that we needed support for a child care center. I noted that he had signed a bill that would bring needed funds to childcare centers and thanked him and gently said that we had not received any money yet. He turned to his aide and said, "How can that be? I signed that bill quite awhile ago." Within three weeks, we had a check. Nobody did anything wrong; it's just that you have to work hard to get things through the pipeline. There should be a person in schools designated to track Federal and state money and prepare a grant request. The best request is done in person.

There was another interesting discovery about providing childcare for mainly single-parent moms. We got the childcare going, but the mothers couldn't get a job because they didn't have any skills to qualify for an office job, which is what they wanted. IBM sent us some computers so we could teach them basic Word and Excel. Parent-teacher associations work hard to improve schools, but so, I've concluded the overall problem is so big that they are not staffed to tackle it.

The political term *limits* is something that has to be fixed. I watch some politicians, and I wonder if they have a pulse. I worked closely with a congresswoman, Naomi Matusow, who was great. We were on opposite ends of the political spectrum, but she listened and was very responsive and interested in problems and I always valued her counsel. Today we would probably have a fist fight. One time, when we were having coffee, she said, "One of my biggest problems is that I was just elected and already I have to plan the fundraising because I'm up for reelection in two years." On the flip side, we have the politician who gets reelected no matter what. Somewhere in the process, they should be asked to sign a covenant agreement that states what he or she will accomplish. And then grade that covenant agreement and publish the report card. Once again, I would assemble a team of corporate people. They know how to do these things. Unions have contacts review the findings with them and move forward *as a team of concerned Americans.*

A lot of people to care for

I hope my book has given you food for thought. Don't be afraid to think outside the box. Change has never been brought about by people who have remained silent and sat around grumbling.

 Mr. Fulton has traveled around the world and has seen firsthand the things that divide us and bring us together. As a deacon in the Episcopal Church, he served as chaplain to the recovery teams after 9/11 and saw the consequences of hate. Taking a paid leave of absence from IBM, he helped set up the first center for families and individuals impacted by HIV/AIDS in Northern Westchester County, New York.

Working with kids who are incarcerated, Mr. Fulton has talked to 2,500-plus kids and understands what racism and poverty do to a person and how it is passed down from generation to generation. His first book, *Yo God, What the Hell*, gave a platform for these kids to be heard.

Mr. Fulton founded the Brieant Youth Alliance in Ossining, New York. He has been honored for his work by his hometown of Somers, New York, Westchester County, Church of the Good Shepherd, Ossining Schools, Brieant Youth Alliance, and numerous IBM awards.

CPSIA information can be obtained
at www.ICGtesting.com
Printed in the USA
BVHW090821091121
621087BV00022B/532